# Hank

An "Angel Dog"

by

David O. Scheiding

**DORRANCE**
PUBLISHING CO
EST. 1920
PITTSBURGH, PENNSYLVANIA 15238

Dorrance Publishing Co
585 Alpha Drive
Suite 103
Pittsburgh, PA 15238
Visit our website at *www.dorrancebookstore.com*

ISBN: 978-1-4809-1972-3
eISBN: 978-1-4809-2087-3

I would like to dedicate this book

to the memory of Hank,

with whom God blessed our family

for fifteen years and seven months.

# Acknowledgments

I would like to thank the following people for all of their help with this book. I want to thank my wife of fifty-two years for putting up with me and helping me, her dumb fighter pilot and engineer husband, to actually write a book. I also need to thank my son, Doug Scheiding, for helping me put the manuscript and photos into digital format. I am also truly indebted to Ms. Mary Jo Salas, who word processed the manuscript on her own time. I also want to thank all the people who encouraged me to write this book and especially Dr. Loretta Ehrlund, D.V.M., who provided the best care possible to Hank. And last but not least, I especially appreciate the staff of Dorrance Publishing Co, for giving me the opportunity to tell the story of Hank.

# Contents

# Prologue

Over the years, there have been many stories written about dogs, stories like *Old Yeller, Lassie,* and many, many more. All of these stories are about remarkable dogs; however, I do not know if there has ever been a more remarkable dog than the one described here.

This is a true story of Hank—our dog, an "Angel Dog." I say dog, but no one will ever be able to convince me that he was just a dog. He truly was an "Angel Dog," placed here on Earth by God to provide the kind of love, comfort, and loyalty that truly expresses God's love for all of his creation. Hank was definitely part of God's plan for our family.

Hank's actions over his fifteen-plus years with our family portrayed that his life was truly guided by a higher power. He was not like ordinary dogs. He did not bark unless he was communicating with humans, nor did he dig, chew, or jump on people or get into things that did not belong to him. It is my belief that only an "Angel Dog," whom God created for a specific purpose, can explain just how remarkable Hank was. This was depicted by his life.

# Introduction

**H**ank joined our family on May 24, 1999. That was the day that my mother-in-law, Mary Dearixon, passed away. Mary was Herman Dearixon's wife and my wife, Jan's, mother. Mary had been fighting lung cancer for a period of time, and the family had gathered in Council Bluffs, Iowa, due to her failing health. Jan and I were in from San Antonio, Texas, while Byron Dearixon (Herman and Mary's son) and his wife, Barbara, were in town from Houston, Texas. Byron and Herman had been looking for a dog for Herman for quite some time. Herman had always had dogs and other animals when he and Mary lived on their farm just outside Council Bluffs. After Mary and Herman both retired, they decided to move into Council Bluffs to enjoy their golden years. Herman had not had a dog since they had moved to town. Herman was one of those people who had a special way with all animals and could train them to do just about anything he wanted them to do. In fact, he was so good at training dogs, an Englishmen had offered Herman a job in England just to train dogs for him. However, if you knew Herman, England was not the place for him. Just getting to England would have been an almost impossible task since Herman would become physically sick to his stomach just thinking about flying. He was not convinced that airplanes actually could fly, even though I was an Air Force pilot.

On that day in May 1999, Herman and Byron were coming back from Omaha when Byron mentioned to Herman that, in their search for a dog, they had not checked the Omaha dog shelter. Consequently they proceeded to Omaha to see what was available.

After looking over all of the dogs present in the shelter, Herman had found a Border Collie that he liked while Byron had found a mixed-breed white dog with a large black patch of hair around his right eye. Byron began to work with both dogs to determine which one would be the best for Herman. Byron is also very good with animals and comes by it naturally. After working with both dogs, Byron felt that the white dog with the black patch around his right eye was the one they should get, and after some discussion, Herman agreed. When asked later what had convinced Byron that the white dog was the one, Byron said this dog obeyed him and did what he wanted him to do. Byron and Herman brought the white dog home, and Mary passed away that afternoon.

We all felt this white dog had been provided by God to be an "Angel Dog" to help Herman get through the rough times ahead. This dog reminded us all of the movie *Dancing with the White Dog.* This movie was about a white dog that became a companion to a man who had just lost his wife. Was this just a coincidence, or was a higher power watching over all of his creation? The next fifteen years provided the answer to this question.

# Chapter 1

# The Beginning

Herman's veterinarian told us the white dog was approximately six to eight months old at the time Herman and Byron picked him out. He was essentially all white with the exception of the black patch around his right eye. He also had a smaller black spot just behind his left eye. His soft velvet-like ears also had small black spots on them. In addition, he had a few small black spots on his body and legs but was primarily white. His eyes were dark brown. He had one black eyelash and one white eyelash (see photo 1). He looked a lot like "The Little Rascals'" dog or the dog on the old RCA record label. His ears did suggest that he might be part Dalmatian; however, our veterinarian later indicated most emphatically that "he was *not* a Dalmatian—not with his temperament!" She felt he was part boxer and some kind of hunting dog. This was supported by his cropped tail. She actually seemed miffed that we would suggest he was part Dalmatian. Our veterinarian, Dr. Loretta Ehrlund, immediately fell in love with him on our first visit to see her. Dr. Ehrlund became a prime figure in our new dog's life after he came to live with us.

My wife, Jan, stayed in Council Bluffs with Herman for a while after Mary's funeral to help him adjust to the change. One of the first tasks to be accomplished was to determine a name for the white dog.

One evening, Jan and Herman were watching a program on television about a couple and their dog. Jan said the couple was pretty sickening by the manner in which they spoke to each other, but their dog, whose name was Hank, was the star of the show. Almost simultaneously at the end of the program, Jan and Herman looked at each other and said, "Hank." On that day, the white dog became "Hank."

# Chapter 2

# Hank and Herman

After all of the family members had departed for their homes, Hank and Herman began adjusting to the changes in both of their lives. Herman had very poor eyesight and was very hard of hearing. What Herman needed was a dog that would be both his eyes and ears, so this began the task of training Hank.

It was not long before Herman found out that Hank had evidently been abused during his initial six to eight months of life. If Herman picked up a broom or any long-handled object, Hank would cower down, thinking he was going to be beaten. Herman knew he would have to help Hank reestablish trust in humans if Hank was ever going to be his eyes and ears. Rebuilding this kind of trust is one of the hardest things to do for a dog six to eight months old, once the abuse has been ingrained in the animal. If anyone could do it, it was Herman, and so the training began. It was also evident that the abuser had been a male since Hank did not cower down when females were around—only males.

Herman's neighbors told us that for weeks, every day, Herman would walk around the backyard with a broom, hoe, or shovel on his shoulder with Hank walking at his side. He did this day after day until he convinced Hank that he was not going to be beaten with the object. Hank was perfect for Herman because Herman now had a purpose and a focus to help him deal with the recent loss of his wife. God knew what Herman needed and had sent Hank as an "Angel Dog" to be his companion to assist him with his loss.

All of Herman's previous dogs had been outside dogs. Hank started out that way, but it was not long before that changed. For the first time in his life, Herman bought Hank a doghouse. He placed it outside by the back porch and even put some straw and hay inside it to keep Hank warm in the winter. It does get pretty cold in Iowa during the winters. However, as the days and weeks passed, it became obvious to Herman that Hank did not like rain, snow, or cold weather. It was not long before Hank was allowed to spend the night inside on Herman's enclosed side door porch. This was also a first for Herman. Hank just had a way of getting into your heart, which led him to get what he wanted. Then it was not too long until Hank was allowed into the kitchen and then the living room. Then another first occurred: Herman went out and bought Hank a pad to sleep on in Herman's bedroom at night (see photo 2). Herman had reestablished Hank's trust, and Hank had stolen Herman's heart. Hank had gone from a timid, stray dog to Herman's first inside dog in a matter of a few months (see photo 3).

During this time period, an extremely strong bond had formed between Hank and Herman. It seemed that all Hank wanted was to be with Herman and do whatever Herman wanted him to do (see photo 4). Hank and Herman became inseparable companions. When Herman would take a nap, so did Hank. If Herman went outside, so did Hank. Hank became Herman's constant companion.

It also was not long before Hank began to go with Herman in his truck on errands. Hank was the first of Herman's dogs to ride inside the truck. All of his other dogs on the farm rode in the truck bed, if they were fortunate to be asked to go. Not Hank; he rode up front inside (see photo 5). If Herman was going someplace that Hank could not go, Herman would leave Hank in the backyard. According to Bill and Mary, Herman's next-door neighbors, Hank would sit in the corner of the backyard watching the street that ran in front of Herman's house, waiting for Herman's return (see photo 6). He would sit there for hours until he would see Herman's truck pull into the driveway. Hank never once tried to jump the fence, which was small, and it would not have been any problems for him to do so. Herman would tell Hank to stay and that he would be back. Hank would wait patiently for his master to return. Hank had no desire to leave.

Hank's presence at home even changed Herman's activities. If the weather was bad, Herman did not go. Even if the weather was good, Herman would leave early from the place he was visiting because he knew Hank was waiting for him at home. Hank gave Herman a new purpose in life. Herman needed Hank, and Hank needed Herman.

Herman continued to train Hank to become his eyes and ears; however, Herman was somewhat concerned because Hank did not bark. This concern disappeared one day when the doorbell rang while Herman was taking a nap. Hank was immediately on duty and began to bark loudly in order to let Herman know someone was at the door. From that day on, Herman knew he had his eyes and ears in Hank.

For five and a half years, Hank and Herman developed an unbelievably close bond of total trust and loyalty. Hank had totally regained his self-esteem and confidence and became totally devoted to Herman. All Hank wanted to do was please Herman. Herman would talk to Hank throughout the day, and Hank would listen intently to try to figure out exactly what Herman wanted him to do. Hank just had to be with Herman no matter which room Herman was in. This was true even when Herman had friends over to the house. Hank would lie in the center of the room and sleep. This was true whether the guests were in the living room or downstairs during a country-western music jam session. All of Herman's friends knew that Hank was inseparable from Herman. Hank was Herman's companion as well as his eyes and ears.

# Chapter 3

# Living with Hank

**B**eing just the two of them, Herman talked to Hank throughout the day. It was not long before Hank began to understand what certain words meant and what actions were desired. Hank began to develop an association between the words and desired actions that Herman was requesting. People say that dogs do not have cognitive thinking capability, but those people never met Hank. Hank's single purpose in life was to please Herman and be his companion. He would constantly watch Herman and listen for any communication from Herman as to what Herman wanted him to do. In addition, since Hank was constantly with Herman, Hank did not need the companionship of any other dogs. Herman was all that Hank wanted or needed. Since Herman was able to reestablish Hank's trust, confidence, and self-esteem, Hank's true personality blossomed forth and was expressed by his facial expressions, actions, and total desire to please. Hank was constantly demonstrating that he was an "Angel Dog" sent by God to comfort Herman.

It became obvious to Herman that Hank was indeed a very special dog. More than once, Herman would comment that he thought Hank may be the smartest dog he had ever seen or had. This is saying something for Herman since he has had dogs that he could send out to a pasture to bring back a specific cow. This is why the Englishman wanted to hire Herman to come to England and train dogs for him. The Englishman had witnessed one of Herman's dogs do that very thing. So for Herman to say that he felt Hank was the smartest dog he had ever had was something very, very special. Hank was being compared to a very large number of dogs and was setting the standard.

Living with Hank was just a real pleasure for Herman. There was not a day that would go by that Hank did not do something that would bring a smile to Herman's face as well as his heart. Hank was truly a blessing and an "Angel Dog."

Hank was always listening and paying attention to what was happening around him and to the activities of Herman and any other humans who might be present. Just by his actions, you could tell Hank was paying attention and thinking all the time. Herman related a story to us about a time when Herman's next-door neighbor's daughter had come home to visit her parents. Bill and Mary were always close to Herman, and they wanted their daughter to meet Herman and Hank. They were all sitting out in Herman's backyard visiting when the daughter decided she wanted to play with Hank. She went back to Bill and Mary's house and soon returned with an old piece of rope to play tug-of-war with Hank. They played for a long time with this rope, much to the delight of Hank. After Bill and Mary and their daughter left, Herman went out to the backyard to retrieve the rope. It was nowhere to be found, so Herman forgot about it. Approximately a year later, when Bill and Mary's daughter returned for another visit, they once again came over to Herman's to visit. They again were all sitting in the backyard visiting when Hank, seeing the daughter, went to wherever he had hidden the old rope and returned it so that she and he could once again play tug-of-war. Herman never did figure out where Hank had hidden the rope, but to Hank, that rope was his and the daughter's toy to play with and no one else's. After all, the daughter had given him that rope to play with—and they say dogs do not have cognitive thinking skills! Herman never saw Hank play with that rope except the two times the daughter came home to visit Bill and Mary. In Hank's mind, that rope belonged to him and her alone. It was their special rope and no one else's.

My wife, Jan, also became aware of how smart Hank was when she was visiting Herman on one of her visits to Iowa. Jan would fix supper for Herman while Hank and Herman were in the living room. When supper was ready, Jan would holler, "Okay!" However, since Herman was hard of hearing, she would have to go into the living room to get Herman. The second night she did the same thing; however, by the third night, when she hollered, "Okay!" Hank got up and immediately sat down in the doorway between the kitchen and living room. Herman had trained him to stay out of the kitchen when

Herman and Jan ate supper. In just three days, Hank had learned that "Okay!" from Jan meant it was supper time.

Hank could sleep a lot. Herman relayed a story about Hank's bed pad that he had gotten Hank to sleep on in Herman's bedroom at night. On one occasion, when Herman had straightened up his bedroom during the day, Herman had placed Hank's pad up against the wall to clean under and around the pad. Hank would sometimes go to bed before Herman. On this night, Herman was sitting in the living room when Hank decided to go to bed. So off to the bedroom Hank went. It was not long before Herman began to hear Hank in the bedroom making all kinds of strange noises. Hank was making noises loud enough for even Herman to hear and know that something was wrong. So Herman got up and went back to the bedroom to see what the problem was. Hank was looking at the pad leaning up against the wall where Herman had left it. Herman placed the pad back down on the floor, and Hank immediately went to sleep. Herman always said, "Hank will let you know what he wants." Herman also would comment that he never saw a dog that could sleep as much as Hank. My wife, Jan, would always remind him that was okay since Hank was always there for Herman as his eyes and ears when needed. He might be sleeping, but he was always on duty. Hank might be sleeping one second but was immediately awake and on all fours if any strange noise would occur.

The loyalty of Hank toward Herman and his assumed duty to protect Herman was very evident one day when Hank and Herman were out in the backyard. A raccoon had entered the yard just inside the back fence. Hank watched this raccoon as it walked along the fence. As long as the raccoon was not moving toward Herman, Hank just stayed by Herman's side. However, the raccoon made a fatal mistake when it turned toward Herman. Hank immediately sprang into action and went after the raccoon. Hank was not going to allow the raccoon to get close to Herman. With one bite on the neck, the raccoon was history. Hank was not going to allow anything to harm Herman on his watch.

On another occasion, two individuals rang Herman's doorbell. Hank began to bark, letting Herman know someone was at the door. As Herman opened the door to see who was there, Hank stood right behind Herman. The two individuals who were at the door were dressed in long black trench coats. These coats did not seem to fit the warm weather of the day. After a short conversation, Herman told the two individuals that he was not interested and started to close the door. One of the individuals stuck his foot in the door to stop Herman from closing the door. Big mistake! Hank sprang into action and lunged around Herman toward this individual. Seeing Hank, this individual decided it was not such a good idea to stop Herman from closing the door. Both individuals immediately turned around and started to run down the driveway with their trench coats flopping in the wind and Hank about two steps behind them. Herman let Hank go until they reached the end of the driveway, when Herman hollered, "Hank!" who immediately stopped, sat down, and watched the two unsavory individuals continue to run away. Needless to say, these two individuals never returned. These two individuals had just met Hank. Herman felt these two individuals did not have any good intentions based on their dress and actions.

Based on the raccoon and this incident, Herman knew that Hank was not only his eyes and ears but also his protector. It has been said that "A dog loves you more than his own life." Hank was a prime example of this.

Even though Hank did not need any other dogs to play with or have as a companion since he had Herman, Bill, Herman's next-door neighbor, told us that Hank did have a visitor come by occasionally. Sometimes when Herman was gone and Hank was in the backyard, a big brown fuzzy dog would come by to visit Hank. The brown dog would jump the small fence to get into Hank's backyard. Bill said that Hank and this dog would play for a long time. When they both got tired, the brown dog would again jump the fence and be on his way. Bill said this happened several times. After the brown dog left, Hank never once tried to jump the fence to follow. Hank knew his place and his duty was to Herman. God had arranged for Hank to be with Herman, and Hank had no desire to leave.

It was on one of our trips to Iowa to see Herman when one day, Herman and I were sitting in the living room talking. Of course, Hank was on the floor between us, sleeping. On that day, I happened to mention to Herman that if for any reason he could not take care of Hank, Jan and I would be very happy to do so. We knew that Byron's wife, Barbara, would not allow Byron to have a dog the size of Hank to come and live with them. Byron had just built his wife a new home. The home looked like something out of *Better Homes and Gardens*—a very beautiful home. We also knew that Herman had given one of his dogs away to a friend on a farm and the dog had gotten killed by a car. Herman always felt bad about that and never forgot it.

After Hank had been with Herman for about five and half years, Herman came to the realization that he would not be able to keep his house up much longer due to his age and health. He realized it was about time to move into an independent living facility. The place he was considering did not allow pets, especially the size of Hank. So one day, Herman called us and asked to speak to me. When I got on the phone, Herman asked, "Dave, do you still want Hank?" There was absolutely no hesitation on my part or my response. It was a definite "Yes!" with the promise to Herman that I would take very good care of Hank. I was aware of the time when he had given a dog to his friend on the farm and the dog was killed. I knew that Herman wanted to be sure that Hank would have a good home. Herman knew that Jan and I would take very good care of Hank. Both Jan and I knew what a special dog—an "Angel Dog"— Hank was. We felt honored that Herman would choose us to take care of Hank. I also feel that God was again directing Hank's life since he was an "Angel Dog" and was taking care of Hank.

On Thanksgiving Day in 2004, we moved Herman into Bethaney Heights, an independent living facility in Council Bluffs, Iowa. That was the day Hank came to live with us. This was an extremely difficult time for Herman since he was giving up his closest friend and companion since the loss of his wife. As we put Hank into the back seat of our truck for the trip to Texas, Herman could not come over to the truck. He just stood in front of the truck, looking down at the ground. I think Hank also knew a change was occurring by his actions. Herman told us that he had a talk with Hank to let him know he was going to be living with us. Hank seemed to know and, although not pleased about it, seemed to accept the change and hopped in the back seat of the truck without hesitation. Since Herman had talked to Hank, there was no doubt in my mind that Hank did understand what Herman had told him, and he knew he had to accept it.

# Chapter 4

# The Trip to Texas

Since Herman had taken Hank with him in his truck on every opportunity he could, Hank thoroughly enjoyed riding in trucks. We had prepared a place for him in the back seat, and he immediately got in, laid down, and went to sleep. We left Council Bluffs the day after Thanksgiving 2004 on our way home to Texas. We normally drove to Ardmore, Oklahoma, the first day of our trip home, where we stayed the night. We arrived in Ardmore that night and checked into a motel. We brought the pad that Herman had bought for Hank to sleep on and placed it on the floor in the motel room. We asked Herman how we would know when Hank needed to go outside to potty. Herman just smiled and said, "He will let you know what he needs." (We did not know just how true this statement was.) Sure enough, it was not long before Hank went to the door of the motel room to go out and potty. This occurred right after I had fed him. We had brought the rest of the dog food that Herman had been feeding Hank. We wanted as few changes as we could to help Hank adjust to life with us. We even brought his doghouse, which he never used while with Herman, nor with us. Hank made it very clear that he needed to go outside, so outside we went.

It was dark, and there were some thunderstorms off to the west of Ardmore. At first, there were just flashes of lightning off in the distance. Hank was snooping around, looking for the exact spot to do his business, when the first small clap of thunder occurred. Hank stopped, looked up at me, and waited for me to say something. Since the storm was quite a distance away, I told him it was okay and to go potty. He did, and after finishing his business, the second clap of thunder occurred. This one was much louder, indicating the storm was rapidly moving our way. With this clap of thunder, Hank looked up at me and immediately started back to the motel room. In his mind this was not okay, and he wanted back in the motel room.

Once in the room, the thunder became much louder and more frequent. Hank seemed to be very concerned about the thunder and became very nervous. He looked around the room and went over to what was Jan's side of the bed. Her side was next to the wall, and Hank lay down between the bed and the wall, trembling, and looking up at Jan for help. Jan began talking to Hank, trying to calm him down. That was when we discovered that Hank was afraid of thunder. He was shaking and looking up at us for comfort. He just did not understand where that thunder was coming from. To the day he left us, thunder always caused the same reaction in Hank.

At our house, Hank would immediately go to the area between Jan's side of the bed and the wall. The layout of our bedroom was similar to that of the motel room we had stayed in at Ardmore. In addition, when we knew a thunderstorm was approaching, we would place Hank's pad there for him to lie on. The only thing that helped Hank deal with thunder was when he started losing his hearing as he got older. At the end, the thunder had to be very loud for him to hear it.

On that trip home to Texas, we learned a lot about Hank. We learned that he really enjoyed riding in a truck. He never caused us any problems during the two-day trip back to Texas, as he slept most of the time. He got out when we stopped at rest areas, and the rest of the time he just slept in the back seat. We also learned that Hank was afraid of thunder. He had a great fear of thunder, which was almost unnatural. He never really got over this fear, but it did moderate as he lost his hearing.

Jan and I both came to believe this fear of thunder was probably the reason Hank got lost in the first place when he was a puppy. We felt that when he was small, a thunderstorm came and he was not in a confined area, so he started running away from the thunder. We felt that he kept running until he could no longer hear the noise. By that time, he became lost and did not know where his home was. We always felt that he had belonged to someone since his tail had been cropped and he obviously had been abused by a male. Due to his extreme fear of thunder, Hank probably became lost and was picked up and taken to the Omaha shelter. One also has to wonder if this was not God's plan for

Hank to ensure Hank was available for Herman when needed in order for Hank to fulfill God's plan and purpose as an "Angel Dog."

Because of this possible scenario, we felt this was also the time Hank began to dislike rain. He did not like to get wet or be outside when it rained. Herman also told us that Hank did not like snow. Coming to Texas allowed Hank to get away from snow for the most part, but he still had to deal with thunder and rain.

While he lived with us, Hank was always inside during thunderstorms. In fact, the only time Hank was outside was when we were with him. When thunderstorms did come, Hank always had his safe place to retreat to until the storm had passed.

# Chapter 5

# Our Life with Hank

There was not a day that went by that Hank did not do something that made us laugh and bring smiles to our faces. He continually reminded us just how special he really was. He was such a remarkable dog, and he did not have any problems adjusting to life with us. Jan and I know that Hank did understand when Herman had his talk with him to let him know he was going to come and live with us. For nine years and five months, he blessed our lives on a daily basis with his devotion and presence just like he did for Herman. He was truly an "Angel Dog"—a gift from God.

When we got Hank on Thanksgiving Day in 2004, Jan was already retired. This was good for Hank since he was used to having Herman around all the time. I was still working, but Hank bonded with me as well as with Jan. He always liked women and kids but was a little leery of men. However, Hank accepted me even though I had not been around him that much. He just seemed to know after Herman had the talk with him that I would take care of him.

Some of the things that made Hank so special and set him apart from most other dogs were that he did not chew on things, he never dug in the backyard, and he never got into things in the house that did not belong to him. He just wanted to please us all of the time just like he had done for Herman. He knew what things were his and just did not get into anything else. Hank just wanted to be with us and do whatever it was that we wanted him to do. He also did communicate with us just as Herman said he would. He would tell us when he wanted to go out, when he was hungry, or when he wanted a drink. We kept his food and water bowls outside, because that was what Herman had done. He also would tell us when he wanted to go for a walk or go in the truck or even when he wanted to play with his toys. He was able to communicate each of these things in such a manner that we knew exactly what he wanted or needed. As Herman had said, "He will let you know." Hank soon became our eyes and ears, as well as our companion, and was truly a member of our family.

For the first five years that we had him, Jan was retired, and she and Hank became very close. She, like Herman, would talk to Hank continually throughout the day. Hank continued to learn the meaning of different words. At one time, Jan started to compile a list of all the words Hank knew, but it soon became too lengthy. Hank knew so many words that Jan and I had to be careful of what we said to each other because Hank was always listening for words that meant he was included in some event. If we happened to forget and say such words as "go" or "are you ready to go?" Hank would immediately get up and head for the door. We had to spell words just to keep Hank from getting too excited about the possibility of him going with us.

During those first five years that Hank was with us, we learned that Hank liked routine. I would get up at 5:30 A.M. to go to work. Hank, of course, slept in our bedroom on his bed. After we brought Hank home with us, I found another pad that matched the pad Herman had bought him (see photo 7). Hank would sleep on these two pads at the foot of our bed. Jan bought beach towels to place over these pads for Hank to sleep on (see photo 8).

Then one day, when I was buying his dog food at the feed store, I found the perfect dog bed for Hank. This bed was a piece of three-inch foam covered with vinyl that also had a sheepskin pillow constructed at one end (see photo 9). I decided to buy it for Hank. The minute I brought this new bed into the house, Hank knew immediately that it was for him. His bed then consisted of the two one-inch foam pads and the new bed on top, all covered with a beach towel. We may have spoiled Hank, but he never took advantage of us. He was always just Hank.

Hank loved his new bed and used it just like humans use theirs. He would sleep on his bed with his head on the pillow portion just like a human. To protect his bed, Jan placed an oversized beach towel over the pads like a bedspread. During the day, Hank would sleep on his bed without messing up the beach towel (see photo 10). However, at night, when we all went to bed, Hank would pull the beach towel back just like we did when we pulled our covers back. He would then lie down on his bed with his head on his pillow and go to sleep (see photo 11).

Hank was very independent. Many times in the evening, when it got to be 8:00 to 8:30 P.M., Hank would get tired and decide to go to bed. He also had a couch bed in the family room, where he slept when we were all in this room (see photo 12). However, at night, when he would get tired, he would leave Jan and me in the family room, and he would go to his bed in the bedroom. As we said, Hank could sleep a lot. As he got older, he slept even more.

When he slept, he looked like a little stuffed animal on his bed; however, he did snore just like an old man. Jan and I liked to listen to him when we went to bed. He would sleep with total trust knowing that no one was going to hurt him, but if there was a strange noise, he was immediately up on all fours, ready for action in case anything was wrong. He was definitely our eyes and ears just like Herman had trained him.

When we traveled, we would take his bed with the pillow built in for him. I would place it on the back seat, where he would sleep as we traveled (see photos 13 and 14). When we would get to the motel or our destination, I would place Hank's bed in a location where I wanted him to sleep. He knew exactly what I wanted with the placement of his bed.

On one trip to Iowa to visit my mother and attend my class reunion, I had placed his bed back in the bedroom where Jan and I were going to sleep. Jan and I were going to one of my class reunion functions, and my mother was going to take care of Hank for us. After we had been gone for a while and while my mother was watching TV, she looked around for Hank. He had been sleeping on the living room floor with her but now was nowhere to be seen. My mother started to panic, not knowing where Hank had disappeared. She got up and began to search the house for Hank. As she searched the house, she finally looked in the bedroom where Jan and I were to sleep. There, to my mother's surprise, was Hank asleep on his bed, where I had placed it. We had forgotten to tell my mother that when Hank got tired, he just went to bed. My mother never forgot about the time Hank went to bed and left her out in the living room.

Since I always got up at 5:30 A.M. to go to work, Hank and Jan would continue to sleep. After I got ready, I would take Hank out the bedroom door to feed him and let him go potty. After he ate and pottied, I would let him back in and he would go back to sleep on his bed. He and Jan would then sleep to 7:30 or 8:00 A.M., when they would get up to start their daily activities.

Hank loved his backyard and considered it his and his alone. He did not like the neighbor's cat or anything else to be in his yard. Each time he went outside, he had to inspect his yard for any trespassers. If anything was present, Hank would take care of them and was extremely fast about it.

On one morning when I let him out, it was still dark. As soon as I opened the door, Hank took off after something that was in the backyard. Before I could say anything, Hank was off the deck and out in the backyard. In a flash, Hank had caught the intruder. However, unfortunately for him and us, the intruder was a skunk. By the time I got outside, Hank was heading back to me with the skunk in his mouth. When I realized what it was by the smell and sight, I hollered for him to drop it. Hank did as commanded and came up to me with yellow spray all over his chest and mouth. He just looked up at me with his big brown eyes that said, "Daddy, help me!" I got Jan up, and we began to try and clean Hank up. This was the only time that Hank did not mind us using water to clean him up. It was about a month later before we finally got the smell off of Hank and out of our bedroom. While we were working on Hank, the skunk got away, and we never saw it again. That skunk had met Hank and did not want any more of him.

On another morning when I let Hank out, he immediately raced across the deck to the barbeque grill. A scuffle immediately occurred between the grill and the deck handrail. Hank was after an intruder. All I could do was hope it was not another skunk. When the scuffle ended, Hank emerged from behind the grill with a possum in his mouth. He was so proud as he brought the possum back to me. I again told him to drop it, which he did at my feet. I got Hank inside the house and then went back outside to get rid of the possum. When I got to the place where Hank had dropped the possum, it was no longer there. I guess that is why they call possums possums. But he too had met Hank and wanted no more.

Jan would get disgusted with me when Hank would go out and catch these varmints until one day when she let Hank out. He immediately raced across the deck after a cat that had entered Hank's territory before Jan could say a word. She learned that Hank was extremely fast when any intruder entered his domain uninvited. Fortunately for the cat, it was able to get over the fence just before Hank could catch it. Nothing was safe in Hank's backyard. This yard belonged to him, and he protected his domain.

Hank really enjoyed his life. He just loved to be with Jan and me no matter what we were doing. His life just revolved around us. After I retired, Hank seemed to enjoy his life even more. Hank's routine changed a little in that we no longer got up at 5:30 in the morning. However, if Hank did not sleep until around 8:00 A.M., when Jan and I would get up, Hank would get me up around 6:30 by coming over to my side of the bed. I would usually hear him shake as he got up just before he came over to awaken me. When I opened my eyes, he would be just standing there, looking at me with his big brown eyes. He had the cutest face that no one could resist. Seeing this face, I, of course, would get up and let him out. If for some reason I did not hear him get up and shake, and his staring at me did not get me to open my eyes, Hank would give me a cute little soft (indoor voice) woof. He used his indoor voice so as not to wake up Jan. How many dogs do you know that understand the difference between an indoor voice and an outdoor voice and when the use of the indoor voice is required? Hank knew and this was not a one-time occurrence. He used his indoor voice many times when Jan was sleeping.

After I would let him out to potty, he would come back to the door, and upon reentry he would come in and go right back to sleep on his bed until around 8:00 A.M., when Jan and I got up to start the day. When Jan and I got up, Hank would just stay on his bed, allowing me time to shave and get ready for the day. He knew he would get to eat after I got dressed. Hank would stay in his bed, watching the bathroom door, waiting for me to come out. However, if it took me longer to get ready than the time Hank thought it should, he would come into the bathroom to check on me to make sure I was on task. He would allow me the amount of time that he considered was enough to get ready.

As long as I was getting ready, he was okay. If I got sidetracked or was talking to Jan, Hank would let me know about it. He would let me know it was time for him to eat. He would do this by trying to herd me to the door. He would get between me and the sink and start pushing me toward the door, just like he was herding sheep.

Hank also knew where I kept his treats, and he got one each morning. As I would go out to the kitchen to get his treat and his food, he would begin to bark (outdoor voice) and let me know he was hungry. He would then run to the back door and wait for me to let him out and feed him.

After he would eat, he would come back into the house and get on his bed. He would then clean himself up and wait for me to wash my hands. Upon completion of our activities, Hank would get up and begin to let me know it was time for his walk. As I put my cap on, Hank would again start herding me toward the door. He would also begin barking (outdoor voice) to let Jan know that we were going for our morning walk. He loved his morning walks in the neighborhood park, which he considered to be his park.

On the way to the park, he would sit in the back seat of the truck, watching to make sure I was going in the right direction. When I would make the turn toward the park, he would get excited and begin to bark, letting me know that I was going in the right direction. We usually had to stop at the traffic light at the park entrance. Hank never really understood why. He would just sit there looking at the park entrance and then look at me as if he were saying, "Daddy, it is right there! Let's go!" He would stick his little mug up next to my ear and give me a loud (outdoor voice) bark. He knew where the park was and could not understand that we had to wait for the light to turn green. Sometimes I would put my hand up on my shoulder, and he would lean forward and lay his mug on my hand. One day when I was busy watching the traffic and he was telling me to go, he laid his muzzle on my shoulder. I had not put my hand up there, so he put his muzzle there anyway. When I did not respond to this, he began to lick the back of my head. He was always doing little things each day that were so special and caused both Jan and me to laugh or at least smile.

Hank knew things and would do things that other dogs just would not do. He seemed to be totally aware of what was going on in his environment and was able to reason what types of actions on his part were appropriate for the existing conditions.

One day, about a year after I retired, Jan did not get up when I got up. This was the first time she stayed in bed sleeping. I got up as usual and went into the bathroom to get ready. Hank stayed on his bed as usual, waiting as I got ready. When I came out to go to the kitchen to get Hank his morning treat and food, Hank followed me out, but he did not bark as he usually did in the mornings. He seemed to know that Jan was still sleeping, and he did not want to wake her. I got his food and he ran to the door as usual, but again, he did not bark as he normally did when Jan was up and awake. Some people would say this was just a coincidence, but I am convinced that Hank was being quiet because he knew Jan was sleeping. Hank was always aware of his surroundings and would adjust his behavior to be appropriate for the current conditions in such a manner that I had never seen before in other dogs. Herman had said that he thought Hank may have been the smartest dog he had ever seen. However, I know for a fact that Hank was the smartest dog I had ever seen!

In addition to his morning walks, Hank loved to ride in the truck. A perfect day for Hank was to sleep to 7:30 or 8:00 A.M., eat breakfast, go for his morning walk, come home and take his morning nap until noon, and then go for a ride in the truck in the afternoon. Upon return, he would take his afternoon nap until 4:00 to 4:30 P.M., at which time he would let me know it was time for him to eat supper. After supper he would sleep in his living room bed until 8:00 to 8:30 P.M., when he wanted to go to bed. Many times I would watch TV in our bedroom while Jan would watch TV in the living room. This caused Hank some concern since he liked us all to be together in the same room. Hank even adjusted to our TV watching routine by adjusting his routine. Hank got so he divided his time up by spending his time with me in the mornings, with both of us in the afternoons, and with Jan in the evenings. Around 9:00 P.M., Jan would usually come back to the bedroom where I watched TV, which made Hank happy. Around 10:00 P.M., I would let him out for the last time for the day. Upon reentry, Hank would get on his bed and be asleep almost immediately, and he normally slept all night.

I mentioned how much Hank loved to ride in the truck. When I was working and Jan would go to Iowa to visit Herman before he passed away, I would take Hank with me to work. If I had a project or job out of town, I would put him in the back seat and off we would go. We would stop at rest areas as needed, and Hank would get out and potty and then get right back in. When we would arrive at the jobsite, Hank would sit in the back seat and watch where I had gone just like he used to sit and wait for Herman to return. When we got back on the road, he would lie back down and sleep. Twice, I took Hank with me to El Paso and back in one day. I would take his food and water on these long trips. It was nineteen hours of traveling to go to El Paso and back to San Antonio in one day. Hank was always ready to go no matter how long it was. He was happy just being with his daddy, and that was all that mattered to him.

In addition to his love of traveling, Hank also loved to play if he saw a purpose in the play event. We bought him toys to play with like Frisbees and ropes to chew on. Jan wanted to play Frisbee with Hank; however, Hank really did not see much of a purpose in Frisbee for him.

After we bought a Frisbee, Jan took Hank out to the back yard to play. To get started, Jan showed Hank the Frisbee and told him he was going to fetch. She tossed the Frisbee and commanded Hank to go fetch. Off he went to retrieve the Frisbee for his master. He immediately brought the Frisbee back to Jan and dropped it at her feet. He was so proud at what he had done! Jan picked the Frisbee up and tossed it again, directing Hank to go fetch. Off Hank went again to retrieve the Frisbee. As before, he returned the Frisbee to Jan's feet and again was so proud! Since the game was going so well, Jan again picked up the Frisbee and tossed it for the third time. Again, off Hank went to retrieve the Frisbee. However, upon returning the Frisbee to Jan, Hank dropped it at her feet as before, but this time, he placed both of his front paws on the Frisbee and looked up at Jan as if to say, "I have brought this back to you three times, and all you do is throw it again. I have had enough." That was the end of the Frisbee game. The ropes are another story, and I will cover them a little later.

Since Hank loved to travel so much, we always took him with us to Iowa to visit Herman. I would fix Hank's bed in the back seat of the truck so that he could sleep while we traveled, and he would have it when we spent the nights away from home. Hank was always ready to go, and he never caused us any problems while traveling. He was just happy to be with us. It also worked out well in that we could take Hank back to Iowa to visit Herman. It was good for Herman to see Hank, and it was good for Hank to see Herman.

On our first trip back to Iowa to visit Herman, I had placed Hank's bed on the floor in Herman's apartment. When Herman saw Hank's bed with the built-in pillow, he just looked at it and smiled. He knew he had made the correct decision when he asked us to take care of Hank. Hank was once again the center of attention in Herman's living room lying on his bed.

After we had been there for a couple of hours talking, Hank got up and went over to Herman, placed his head on Herman's thigh, and looked up at Herman as if to say, "I still remember you." This was a moment none of us will ever forget, and the smile on Herman's face was priceless (see photo 15). It was totally obvious that Hank remembered Herman, yet some say dogs do not have cognitive thinking skills.

Herman was able to see Hank four or five times before he passed away in 2009. Hank always remembered Herman. Each time we visited, Hank would go over to him at some point and look up at him as if to say, "I will never forget you" (see photo 16). This always got to us, and I know how happy this made Herman (see photo 17).

In 2010, Jan and I took a vacation to Oregon to attend a family reunion on Jan's side of the family. It was set up by a sister of Herman's when the family gathered for Herman's funeral in 2009. Of course, Hank was going to go.

Once again, I prepared Hank's bed in the back seat of the truck. We knew that Hank would not be a problem on the trip. He would travel all day and many times well into the night with never a peep out of him. He was always such a pleasure to travel with. There was only one time during the return trip home when Hank had some concern. On our way back to Texas, we decided to return through Colorado and the Rocky Mountains. It was on a day when we were in the mountains that Hank let us know we were high enough in altitude. We were going through a mountain pass that was eleven thousand feet in elevation when Hank stood up in the back seat and looked out the window. We were going through a pass that had a sheer drop-off next to the road with no guardrails present. It was a sheer drop off the mountain side. Hank looked at this drop-off, turned around, and buried his head in his beach towel that was on his bed as if to say, "Daddy, this is high enough! Let's go down." Thankfully, and ironically, this was the highest point of the pass. Hank knew we were very high in altitude, and he was letting us know that as far as he was concerned, we were high enough. Jan and I agreed, and we were happy that we were starting back down ourselves. When we stopped at a rest area later, we checked the map. The place where Hank decided we were high enough was the highest point. Hank knew it and decided that was indeed high enough.

After two weeks of traveling and ten thousand miles later, we arrived home. Hank immediately got back into his routine as if nothing had happened, but I know if asked, he would have been ready to go again. Hank just loved to travel, and it was such a pleasure to take him, although he would just as soon not go back to the mountains.

Hank was just a very special dog. His veterinarian in San Antonio noticed it the first time she met him. After we got him, we took him in to get his shots and nails trimmed. Upon our arrival, the technician took us back to one of the exam rooms, where a large stainless-steel lift table was present. They placed large dogs on this lift table so that the dogs could be raised up for the vet to examine. The technicians had Hank get on this table and then began to put a muzzle on him and secured his head with the muzzle rope to the back of the table. Hank did not understand why his head was being restrained or why a muzzle had been placed on him. After a couple of minutes, the vet (Dr. Loretta Ehrlund) entered the room and approached Hank. She immediately said, "He doesn't need this!" (She was referring to the muzzle.) She knew immediately just by looking at Hank that he would not try to bite her. She and Hank developed a very special relationship over the years. In fact, over the nine-plus years that she was Hank's vet, she saved his life at least three times.

The first time she saved his life occurred when we noticed Hank just did not seem to feel very well. He was not acting like the Hank we knew. This had been going on for a couple of days. He was very lethargic and just laid around all of the time. He had no interest in his food. When Hank stopped eating, we knew something was wrong.

We took Hank in to see Dr. Ehrlund. She examined him very carefully and then said she wanted him to get an ultrasound exam of his stomach. She had noted something that should not be there. She said this would determine what was inside Hank and what could be done if anything. She set up the exam appointment at a location across town that specialized in these types of services. Jan immediately took Hank to this appointment. After Dr. Ehrlund got the results, she immediately scheduled Hank for surgery. It was obvious by Hank's condition that he did not have much longer to live unless there was an intervention. He had not eaten for three days. Dr. Ehrlund kept Hank overnight and operated on him the very next morning.

After the operation, Dr. Ehrlund called and said we could come by to see Hank. When we got to her office, Dr. Ehrlund asked us if Hank ever chewed on anything. We told her that Hank never chewed on things, but sometimes I would play tug-of-war with a rope with him. The rope we played with had two very large knots, one on each end of the rope. However, I always put the rope away after we finished playing. When we would play with the rope, he liked to chew on the knots. I had to watch him because he would chew on the rope until pieces would come off. I watched him so that he did not swallow any of these pieces. When the rope would get too bad, I would throw it away.

Since Hank never got into anything that was not his, I did not think anything about throwing the old ropes away in a wastepaper basket in our bathroom. Hanks always had access to this room; however, he had never taken anything out of the basket before. When we went to see Hank after his operation, Dr. Ehrlund was standing there with a plastic bag with what she had removed from Hank's stomach. Inside this bag was one of the two large knots off the end of the rope that I had thrown away (see photo 18). Hank, thinking the rope was his, saw nothing wrong with his retrieving it from the trash while we were away. Somehow he was able to swallow the whole knot, which was the size of a lemon. To this day, I have no idea how he was able to swallow that knot without choking himself to death. But there it was, in the plastic bag, and Dr. Ehrlund had removed it from the intersection of his stomach and his intestine. It was so big that it was blocking the entrance to his intestine, and it was just a matter of time before Hank would have died. Dr. Ehrlund had saved Hank's life!

Hank had never gotten into the wastepaper basket before, nor had he since this incident. In his mind, the rope belonged to him and he saw nothing wrong if he played with it while we were away. Needles to say, that was the end of ropes for Hank!

During his recovery from this incident, Hank captured the hearts of all of the staff who worked for Dr. Ehrlund. He became one of their favorite patients. After this incident, Hank always looked forward to visiting the vet because he got to see all of his friends who had taken very special care of him. The muzzle and restraint were never seen or mentioned again.

John, one of Dr. Ehrlund's technicians, trimmed Hank's nails. I could not do it because it would have broken my heart if I quicked him. Dr. Ehrlund said she could not trim her dog's nails, either. We would take Hank in to see John every three or four weeks to get his nails trimmed. When Hank got his nails trimmed, John would get down on the floor with him to do it. No more lift table for Hank. After finishing trimming Hank's nails, John would give him treats. I do not think they gave treats to all of their patients, but Hank was always able to talk John out of three or four treats each time. Then, when we would go up front to pay for his nail trim, other technicians would be up front to greet him, and they and the receptionist would also give him treats. Needless to say, Hank liked to go to the vet. John has said that Hank was his favorite patient. It was obvious by their actions that Dr. Ehrlund and her staff all loved Hank. He just had a way of stealing your heart.

You could tell that Dr. Ehrlund loved Hank by the way she looked at him. When we would take Hank in to see her, she would always say, "Let's see what we can do for Hank," as she would enter the exam room. The expression on her face gave away about how she felt about Hank. She also would get down on the floor with him. No more steel lift table for Hank with her, either.

When she got down on the floor, Hank would bury his head in her lap. Hank seemed to know that Dr. Ehrlund had saved his life. In addition, anytime we would talk about Hank with Dr. Ehrlund, she would always take his side. One day we commented to her that Hank really loved to go for walks in the park and how much he loved to travel. While we were talking, she was scratching Hank behind his ears. She just smiled and kept on scratching and said, "They like to do things, too." She was never in a hurry when treating Hank.

On another occasion, we asked Dr. Ehrlund if we should be giving Hank baths. Since Hank hated to get wet, we felt we should ask her about this subject since we had not given him any baths. She responded by looking at him and asked us if he was keeping himself clean, which he did. We responded with a "yes." Again, taking Hank's side, she said that Hank did not need to take baths. As such, Hank never had a complete bath. He did have a partial bath the time he caught the skunk. Hank did make an exception that time.

When other people would meet Hank, they also seemed to sense that he was an exceptional dog. It seemed that anytime he met someone new, he would always get a compliment. People in the park, especially women, would comment on what a "beautiful," "handsome," or "cute" dog he was. They would stop us and ask what kind of dog he was. It would just melt their hearts when we told them that Hank came from a shelter. After we would tell them about his time with Herman, they would just look at him as if they could tell that indeed he was an "Angel Dog."

We continued to go to Iowa to visit my mother, who lived in Marshalltown, Iowa. However, in 2008 we had to move her to an assisted living facility also. Since Herman really liked Bethaney Heights, we decided to move my mother from Marshalltown to Council Bluffs, where Herman was. This was good for a number of reasons. We were able to visit both of them at the same time, and my mother had Herman there to help her adjust to the move. Of course, each time we visited we took Hank.

When Herman moved into Bethaney Heights, they had a restriction of "no pets." However, when we moved my mother in, they had changed their restriction to allow pets that weighed twenty-five pounds or less. Hank, of course, exceeded this restriction also. However, since the staff at Bethaney and many of the residents there knew that Hank used to be Herman's dog, Hank was always welcomed at Bethaney.

On one visit to Iowa, I had to walk past the Bethaney director's office to see the nurse. I was a little concerned because Hank was with me. The director had someone in her office as Hank and I walked by. On the way out, we had to pass by her office again. I thought I was in trouble when she hollered to me, "Bring that dog in here!" When we entered her office, she immediately got up from her desk, came around to Hank, and started petting him and talking to him. She wanted to see Hank since she knew that Hank used to be Herman's dog. Herman was a favorite at Bethaney Heights, so Hank was always welcomed to visit. In fact, when we would plan to visit Herman and my mother, we would inform Bethaney when we were planning to be there. Upon acknowledgement of our plans to visit, the assistant director would always email us back with, "Bring Hank!" There was just something special about Hank that everyone saw in him. One of the other residents at Bethaney would go out of her way to buy Hank treats when we visited. People just knew that Hank was a special dog.

We, like Herman, modified our activities because of Hank. We did not like to go places where we would be gone for any length of time if Hank could not go with us. We always tried to take Hank with us. Hank was so special, and it was a privilege to be able to take care of him. Our activities were influenced greatly by Hank since Hank's world revolved around us. He just wanted to be with us.

As I mentioned before, not one day would go by without Hank doing something that would bring a smile to our faces. Even with all the attention he received, he did not act spoiled and remained "just Hank." Each time I fed him, he would look up at me with his big brown eyes as if to thank me for his food as I placed it in his bowl. He also was very gentle when taking food or treats out of my hand. He was so careful so as not to hurt me.

Many times at night when we were all going to bed, I would get down on the floor while Hank was on his bed. During these times, Hank would begin to lick my hands as if he needed to clean me up. It was almost biblical in nature as when Jesus washed his disciples' feet. Hank thought he had to wash his daddy's hands as if to thank me for taking care of him. He would really concentrate on this task and was very thorough with his cleaning.

Hank also liked to be "loved on" in the mornings after we all got up. Both Jan and I would get down on the floor while he was on his bed to pet him and rub his tummy. He just loved this attention. He also liked to touch us while we loved on him. While we petted him, he would place his paw on our hand or foot if we happened to be standing next to him. Also, when Jan would get near him, his little stub tail would start to wag. His little tail would always give him away. It has been said that a dog wags his tail with his heart. It sure was true for Hank. He also liked it when Jan would sing to him. Hank really enjoyed every moment of his life and was a true blessing to us.

As I mentioned, Hank had his way of communicating with us. One morning after we had returned from his morning walk, Hank once again did something that brought a smile to our faces. What Hank usually did when we returned from his walk was get a drink, and then he would go inside the house and just flop down on his bed. He would get tired from his walk and would just want to get back to his bed. On this particular morning, Jan had not gone on the walk with us. When it was cold, Jan did not go with us. On this day, after I had let him back in and he flopped down on his bed, he seemed to be watching me. Jan and I were talking when Hank got up, came over to me, and looked up at me with his big brown eyes. He seemed to be thanking me for taking him for his walk. He then went back to his bed and lay back down. Jan and I both knew he was indeed thanking me for taking him on his walk. Hank had his own way of thanking us for the things we did for him. It was just like Herman had said: "He will let you know."

Hank was so smart that he knew when he could bark and when he should not. At home, as I mentioned earlier, he would let me know when he was hungry and it was time for him to eat. When it was time to eat, he would get up from his bed in the living room and give me a loud woof. I would get up and head to the kitchen, where I kept some of his food. Hank would then run to the door while barking. However, as I mentioned earlier, when Jan was sleeping, Hank did not bark. He also knew that when we were traveling and we were in the motel, he should not bark. At feeding time in the motel, he would follow me around the room and look up at me when it was time to eat. He would not bark, but he did let me know that he was hungry. He also seemed to know that it was okay when other people in the motel were making noises that he did not have to bark. If people were talking while walking past our door or making noises while entering their rooms close to us, he would just lie on his bed and look up at us with his ears at attention, but he would not bark. How he knew the difference, I will never know. Somehow he did know when he could or should bark and when he should not. He was just a pleasure to travel with and never caused any problems.

We bought Hank a harness to take him for his walks in the park each day. The harness fit over his head and chest, and he had to step into it with his two front paws. The leash attached to the harness and secured him by his chest, thereby not putting stress on his neck or collar. The force to hold him on the leash was absorbed by his chest and not his neck. The harness also had a loop on it that I could use to strap him in using the backseat seatbelts while we traveled (see photo 19). In case of an accident, he was restrained and would not be thrown around inside the truck. Hank seemed to know he was safer in the truck with his harness and seatbelts on and never minded me strapping him in.

Each morning when we would get ready to go for his walk, I would put his harness on. He would let both Jan and me know it was time to go. One morning when he was out in the living room looking for Jan to tell her it was time to go for his walk, I went back to the bedroom to get his harness. I was standing by the door, holding his harness down at his level to put it on him. As Hank came running back to the bedroom to tell me he had gotten Jan's attention, and Jan was following him, Hank ran straight over to where I was holding his harness. He stopped running when he stuck his head into the harness and looked up at me as if to say, "Put my feet in." Jan and I both looked at each other and laughed. As I have said, not a day went by that he did not do something that made us laugh.

At the park, there is a green post with green plastic bags and a request to utilize these bags to clean up after pets. We would usually carry three or four bags with us since Hank usually had to go twice while on his walk. Jan would usually carry the bags and clean up after Hank while I held him. He developed a routine that he did not go at home after his breakfast but would go twice at the park. If he did go at home, he only would go once in the park.

The path we usually walked on started at the east end of the parking lot and ended at the west end of the lot. The pole with the green plastic bags was located at the west end. We would carry extra bags in the truck since we were not near the pole when we started our walk and would resupply at the end of the walk. Usually, Hank completed his business right after we started the walk, or at least before we were halfway through. On a day when Jan did not go with us, I did not have any bags with me for Hank. Hank must have known I did not have any bags because he did not go while were walking. As we were ending our walk and were approaching the pole where the bags were located, I decided I would get some extras for the next day. As I stopped to get the bags, Hank decided it was time for him to do his business. So there I was, getting the bags, and Hank was doing his business right beside the pole where the bags were located. As luck would have it, a number of people were watching as Hank completed his business and as I cleaned it up. It was as if Hank knew where the bags were located and waited until we were at this location before he did his business. He made us both look good in front of the people who were observing us.

We have a shade on the back door in our bedroom. During the night, of course, it is down. During the day, we would pull the shade up with the drawstring, which secured to a small hook on the doorframe. We pulled it up during the day so that Hank would not get tangled up in the drawstring. He learned if this shade was down, he could use his nose to flick the shade back and it would lodge on the window frame on the door and he could look out. It only took one flick of his nose to allow him the ability to look outside.

One night when I was in back watching TV, Jan and Hank were out in the living room watching TV. Around 8:00 to 8:30 P.M., Hank got tired and wanted to go to bed. I had lowered the shade since it was dark outside. Jan decided to follow Hank back to see what he was doing. Since Hank was standing by the door, Jan decided she would let him out. Jan was already in her pajamas and wanted to see if the neighbors were out in their backyard. Jan went to the door and pulled the shade back at her eye level to look outside to see if the coast was clear. Well, not to be outdone, Hank decided he would help her check to be sure the coast was clear. Hank used his nose at his level to flick the shade over so that he could also look out. Jan looked at me and said, "I am glad you saw it also." We both were laughing at just what had happened. Hank was helping Jan check out the backyard before the door would be opened. No one else would believe the little things Hank did that indicated just how special he was—except Herman. You just had to live with Hank to really appreciate just how special he was. It was the little things he did that made him so special. He was always doing little things that indicated his whole life revolved around us, and he wanted to be part of everything we did as well as what he did.

After I would feed him at night, he would reenter the house from the back door and run to tell Jan that his "daddy" had fed him. Jan was usually in the kitchen preparing supper when I would feed him. He would literally run through the bedroom and into the living room to tell Jan that he had gotten to eat. It was if he wanted to share his good fortune with Jan.

He would also do the same thing with me if Jan did something for him like letting him out to potty. Upon reentry, Hank would find me to let me know that Jan had let him out and that he had been a "good boy." He just wanted to share everything he did with the both of us. It was very important to him that both of us knew what he had just done. Actions like these convinced us that Hank just wanted to be with us all of the time. He was not that interested in other dogs. We thought back to the days when Hank was with Herman. Herman essentially spent all of his time with Hank, training him and talking to him. Hank did not have a need for other dogs since his companions consisted of Herman and then eventually us. After we got him, Jan was retired and was able to spend her time with Hank. After I retired, we all spent our time together. Not only did Hank's life revolve around us, I have to admit that our lives revolved around him. As we looked back, since the time he was in the shelter, Hank was never around other dogs that much for him to realize that he was a dog. He thought he was a human since that was how he was treated from the time he was six months old. I am not convinced that he was not part human and was trapped in a dog's body. His actions many times were more human than canine. I do know, however, that he was indeed an "Angel Dog."

Hank also seemed to know he was smarter than other dogs. One of our next-door neighbors had three dogs that they just allowed to exist. Each time Hank would go outside in his backyard, these three dogs would run along the fence line that separated our lots, barking like complete idiots. At first, Hank would run along the fence on his side and bark back at them. When he would do this, I would tell him, "We don't talk to them." After two or three times of having this discussion, Hank would just walk over to the fence and then walk very slowly along his side of the fence without barking. He knew he was smarter than them and he would just tease them. I would chuckle at him while I watched him tease these dogs each time he went outside. He knew exactly what he was doing and enjoyed it. At times he would stop, look at me, and then continue his slow walk to torment his dumb dog neighbors next door.

Because Hank's world revolved around us, Hank would always keep track of us while we were home. If Jan or I had to leave for a while and the other stayed home with him, Hank would wait patiently for the other to return. When Jan or I would return, we immediately had a shadow. Hank would follow whoever had just returned, not letting that person out of his sight. He was the happiest when all three of us were together.

After his morning walk, Hank liked to go back to Jan's office with me while I watched TV. Jan had soap operas that she liked to watch in the morning in the living room. When Jan would watch her shows, Hank and I would go back to her office and watch TV back there. We had another bed back there for Hank just like the one in the bedroom.

I would sometimes go back to her office in the afternoon to watch TV. One day when I had been gone to get a haircut, upon my return Hank was doing his shadow act. He was following me all over the house. I had gone back to her office with my shadow right beside me. However, on this day, I decided not to stay back there and I was returning to the living room, where Jan was. As I came out of Jan's office, Hank was leading the way down the hallway at the very moment Jan was coming down the hallway toward us. I stopped and so did Hank. Hank then actually backed up to get closer to me and sat down right in front of me, facing Jan. It was as if he was telling Jan that since I had been gone for a while, "his daddy belonged to him now, and she would have to wait." Jan and I looked at each other and laughed. He had actually backed up without looking and sat down. He knew exactly where I was and that I had stopped. The dog just knew where we were at all times and kept track of us. We belonged to him and not the other way around.

As I previously mentioned, Hank was always doing things that, to my knowledge, other dogs usually did not do. He also was interested in so many things. On one of our trips to Iowa to visit Herman and my mother, he displayed his interest in different things. We were staying at the motel that we always stayed at while we were in Council Bluffs. This motel was the one we liked, and Hank just loved to stay there also. The motel owner also got to know us, and he really liked Hank. He was supposed to charge us ten dollars a day for Hank, but he never did. He, like everyone who met Hank, simply fell in love with him. Over the years we visited in Iowa, the owner had to change his policy about pets. He had to restrict pet size to no larger than twenty-five pounds, but Hank was grandfathered and this rule did not apply to him. You should have seen some of the looks we got when Hank was seen by other guests who had to abide by the rule.

On one of these trips to Iowa, Hank and I were walking around the motel when a grasshopper landed on Hank's nose. Hank stopped and tried to figure out just what this creature was. It soon left his cold, wet nose and landed on the parking lot in front of him. Having lived in Texas for a while, Hank had not seen any grasshoppers up close and personal. As such, he had to investigate this strange creature that had attacked him. As he put his nose down to investigate, the grasshopper flew away. Hank looked up at me with a puzzled look on his face as if to say, "What was that, Daddy?" Since the grasshopper flew away, we continued on with our walk.

As we were finishing up our walk and as we were approaching the front door, the motel owner's wife was sitting out in the front, smoking a cigarette. The motel was a non-smoking motel. She was watching Hank and me as we crossed the parking lot. As we passed behind some of the parked cars, Hank picked up a piece of paper that someone had discarded. Hank kept this piece of paper in his mouth until we got to the front door, where a trashcan was located. Hank dropped the piece of paper in front of this trash and looked up at me. I picked up the paper and threw it away. The motel owner's wife had observed Hank picking up the paper and carrying it to the trashcan. The look on her face indicated just how amazed she was about what she had just seen Hank do! I naturally played it off by saying, "Hank is just helping you keep your parking lot clean." All she could do was smile and stare at Hank. You just had to see the things he did to believe. The motel owner's wife was now a believer.

On another trip to Iowa, Hank and I were again outside the motel, walking along the exterior fence that surrounded the motel. The motel has a large vacant grass/weed-covered lot on one side of the building. Hank really liked this area. Many times in the morning or evenings, Hank would pick up the scent of a rabbit or other creature. Being part hunting dog, he always liked to track down these creatures. It was on one of these walks in the morning when Hank picked up a scent. He began trailing this scent along the fence line that ran in front of the motel next to the highway. After picking up the scent, Hank increased his pace in order to catch up with whatever it was he was trailing. The motel has a lot of windows in front where the lobby is located. As Hank and I were hot on the trail of this varmint, we did not know we had an audience. A number of guests and the motel owner were watching us. The lobby was where motel guests could get a continental breakfast and visit with each other. As Hank and I were tracking down this varmint, we didn't know we were also providing the morning breakfast entertainment. As Hank picked up the pace, I was almost running while holding his leash. When we got to the front of the motel, just in front of us were three baby raccoons. These three baby raccoons began to rapidly climb the fence to get away from Hank. He had picked up the scent that he remembered from the time he had protected Herman in the backyard. Hank ran up to where the baby raccoons were and since they were not threatening me, he was going to let them go. When we entered the motel lobby, everyone was talking about how Hank had not tried to kill the baby raccoons. The motel owner just smiled as Hank and I went to our room. Once again, people were amazed by the actions of Hank.

Hank would have been an excellent hunting dog if Herman would have trained him. However, Herman was well past his hunting days when he got Hank or he surely would have trained him. After my tour in Vietnam, I no longer had any interest in hunting, so I did not try to train Hank to hunt, either. However, his natural instincts always took over when the few opportunities he had to track rabbits occurred.

It was on one of our trips home from Iowa that Hank had one of these opportunities. The motel we stayed at in Ardmore, Oklahoma, had a large vacant tract of land next to it. (We always chose motels to stay in that had lots of grass for Hank.) This vacant lot consisted of two to three acres of grass/weed covering. Hank always liked to visit this vacant lot when we stayed in Ardmore. On this trip, when we were walking in this lot, Hank picked up a scent of a rabbit. He immediately picked up the pace in hopes of catching up to the rabbit. It was not long before Hank surprised the rabbit, and it took off running. I do not think the rabbits that inhabited this vacant lot had many dogs chase them, because the rabbit did not run very far before it stopped. This was great fun for Hank. He stayed on the rabbit's trail and once again flushed the rabbit out. The rabbit again ran a short distance and stopped. This time, instead of me trying to keep up the pace that Hank was setting, I released his leash. Off Hank went at a full run. The rabbit now began to realize that Hank was more than a passing nuisance and began to run longer and in large circles. I watched as Hank continued to trail this rabbit around the vacant lot. Finally, Hank was getting closer to the rabbit, and the rabbit decided it was time to put an end to this torment. A small drainage feature ran through one side of the lot. After running around in larger circles, with Hank getting closer, the rabbit headed for this drainage ditch. The drainage ditch was not visible as a ditch since the weeds had grown up to be at level with the banks of the ditch. I watched as Hank and the rabbit headed toward the ditch at full speed. Then both Hank and the rabbit disappeared from sight. That was when I hurried over to the ditch to see where they had gone. When I got there, Hank was standing in the middle of the ditch, which was about three feet deep, with a puzzled look on his face. He looked up at me with this look as if to say, "Daddy, what happened?" The rabbit had finally eluded Hank and got away. I got Hank out of the ditch, and we went back to the motel. I had to relay Hank's experience chasing rabbits in the vacant lot next door to Jan. We both enjoyed the tale, and Jan wished she had been able to see all the action. Hank was tired and fell asleep on the floor. I am sure he was dreaming of the good time he had chasing that rabbit.

As Hank grew older, he began to mellow. When he was thirteen years old, he seemed to know that he did not have to be on duty all of the time. When we went on his morning walks, he ignored other dogs completely. He then began to greet anyone who came to the house instead of barking at them to let us know they were here. Even on Halloween, he did not bark when the "trick-or-treaters" rang the doorbell. He seemed to know they were kids and not a threat. Even our cleaning ladies would pet him when they came each week. At first, the maids were afraid of him, and we would put him in the bedroom when they arrived. As he got older, the maids enjoyed him and even wanted to pet him when he greeted them at the door with his short tail wagging.

After I retired, Hank just seemed to know that he did not have to be on guard all of the time. However, I knew that if Jan or I expressed any concern about someone at the door, Hank would protect us. Since Hank was always watching us, he took his queues from our actions. Hank had modified his behavior to match our needs.

On July 29, 2012, Hank did one of the most remarkable things I had ever seen a dog do. This involved Hank knowing what things I did around the house and what things Jan did. Jan was reading the paper, and I was watching the Olympics. We were in the living room, and Hank was lying on his bed by the sofa. Jan was usually cold and the one who controlled the thermostat in our household. It was about 2:00 in the afternoon, and it was getting hot outside. Hank lifted his head up from his bed and began huffing and puffing like he normally did around 3:00 P.M. when he was hungry. He then got up from his bed and walked toward Jan along the rug that we had in front of the sofa. I had placed this rug in front of the sofa so that Hank would not scratch Jan's hardwood floors with his nails. He would walk down this rug toward us when he wanted to get our attention. He would then stand there at the end of the rug and look at whichever one of us whose attention he was trying to get. This time he stopped at the end of the rug and looked directly at Jan and barked. Being a little slow, I just assumed he wanted to go outside. Since Jan was reading the paper, I got up to take him out even though he was not looking at me. As I got up and was heading toward the door, Hank just stood there, looking at me and then Jan. After a short pause, Hank did not head for the door, but instead he returned to his bed by the sofa. Since it was only 2:00 P.M., it was not time for him to eat, and he did not seem to want to go outside, so I went back to my chair and sat down. About two or three minutes passed when Hank once again got up and started huffing and puffing as he walked down the rug again toward Jan. He again stopped, looked directly at Jan, and again barked. This time he did get Jan's attention, and when he did, he then looked over to the wall where the thermostat was located. Well, not being as smart as Hank, I missed what he was trying to tell Jan, so I again got up to let him out. Again, Hank walked back to his bed and laid down. However, Jan had noticed that

Hank had looked over to where the thermostat was located and had figured out by his huffing and puffing he was telling Jan that he was hot. Hank knew Jan always set the thermostat and she could make it cooler. Since I was already up, Jan asked me to check the temperature. I did and it was 75 degrees in the house. We learned that when it got to 75 degrees in the house, Hank was hot. I lowered the thermostat to 74 and returned to my chair. Hank returned to his bed but was still looking at Jan. Since it took a little time for the air-conditioning unit to come on, Jan told him it would get cooler soon. When the unit did come on, Hank laid his head down and went back to sleep.

By watching our actions and the different things each of us did around the house, Hank had learned who controlled the temperature. Since he was hot, he communicated his needs to the one person he knew who could fix his problem. I found this incident to be totally remarkable! Many people would not believe us if we told them what Hank had done. However, I know that Herman would believe it since he had lived with Hank and knew what he was capable of. Jan and I again thought back to when Herman had said, "He will let you know."

After that, any time the temperature in the house got to 75 degrees, Hank would start his huffing and puffing, and we both knew what he wanted. At 74 or lower, Hank was content.

# Chapter 6

# The Beginning of the End

On January 31, 2013, we took Hank to Dr. Ehrlund for his annual checkup appointment and shots. After checking him over very thoroughly, we were very happy to get Dr. Ehrlund's report. She said his heart was strong, good lungs, and all of his internal organs seemed to be in very good shape. His weight of sixty pounds was good, and he seemed to be in excellent health for a dog of his size and age. Dr. Ehrlund did note that he had some arthritis in his left-front leg and in both of his back legs. We figured this was normal for a dog of his age. She did recommend, however, that we get his teeth cleaned, and she provided him with some pain pills for his arthritis. We asked Dr. Ehrlund if there was much risk for Hank while cleaning his teeth since we knew he would have to be put under. Dr. Ehrlund explained that any risk was small since the anesthesia she used was very mild like the type used for babies. She asked us when we wanted to make the appointment to get his teeth cleaned. She did have an opening the very next week. This was again where God revealed he was still guiding Hank's life.

Jan and I both like to go to the San Antonio Rodeo. We have season tickets and go to just about every performance. The rodeo runs for approximately two and a half weeks. Since the rodeo was starting in about a week, we decided to postpone his teeth cleaning until after the rodeo. We scheduled Hank's teeth cleaning on February 27, 2013. Jan and I were both very pleased about Hank's report and looked forward to the rodeo.

On February 27, 2013, we took Hank back to Dr. Ehrlund to get his teeth cleaned, nails trimmed, ears cleaned, and have a couple of small tags removed. We got him there between 7:30 and 8:30 A.M. as requested. Jan and I left after the receptionist told us Hank would be ready to come home around 3:00 P.M. We decided to go get breakfast and figure out what other things we could do to help pass the time until 3:00 P.M.

At 2:45 P.M., the phone rang, and the receptionist said that Hank was ready and we could come and get him. Of course, we left right away in order to get him back as soon as possible. When we arrived at Dr. Ehrlund's office, the receptionist said Dr. Ehrlund wanted to talk to us. The receptionist took us back to an exam room to wait for Dr. Ehrlund. This raised our first concern. When Dr. Ehrlund came into the exam room with Hank, we sensed something was wrong by the serious expression on Dr. Ehrlund's face. Hank had always had small fatty lumps on his body that were of no consequence. This time Dr. Ehrlund asked us if we had noticed any lumps on his lymph nodes under his legs. She pointed these lumps out to us, much to our shock. These lumps had not been present on January 31, when she had examined him during his annual checkup. Dr. Ehrlund was also very surprised to find these lumps less than thirty days after his annual checkup. Dr. Ehrlund went on to say that she had already consulted with Dr. Wright, another vet in her office, and they decided to do a biopsy of one of these lumps. The results were very bad news. Hank had developed Stage III Lymphoma in all of his lymph node system. This news was very devastating to Jan and me. We asked Dr. Ehrlund how long Hank had. She said without treatment, it would be four to six weeks. However, she did say "without treatment." We, of course, asked about what treatment was available for Hank. She explained that she could give him chemotherapy treatment similar to human treatment. She went on to say the treatment was expensive, but if the cancer was detected soon enough, they had good results with the thirteen-week treatment schedule. She also gave us some information about lymphoma in dogs and the treatment protocol. She indicated that 75 percent of the time, treatment could extend a dog's life for ten to twelve months. She suggested we go home, read the information, and then call her back after we decided what we wanted to do for Hank. She also said she would have to order the medication since she did not keep it on hand. Neither Jan nor I had to think about it. Whatever the cost, we wanted the treatment for Hank and requested she order the medicine. In the meantime, she gave us some pills for Hank to take as preparation for the treatment. She said the pills would increase his urination, which would help prepare him. We departed her office with a devastating sadness that we had not arrived with.

As we waited for the chemotherapy medicine to arrive, we began to think back, and that was when we realized God had again guided Hank's life. If we could have scheduled Hank for his teeth cleaning the very next week after his annual checkup appointment, Dr. Ehrlund might not have detected his cancer in time to even give him the treatment. God was taking care of our "Angel Dog."

After a couple of days on his new medicine that increased his urination, Hank had an accident on the bedroom carpet. I was in the shower and Jan was in the bathroom when Hank needed to go out. Since he could not find either of us, he had an accident on the bedroom floor. When Jan got out of the bathroom, she found his accident. She also found Hank on his bed with his head down, thinking he was in trouble. It was obvious that Hank felt extremely bad about the accident. Jan cleaned up the carpet while Hank watched her with his sad eyes. Neither of us got after Hank since we could tell he felt really bad, and the accident was not really his fault. Hank stayed on his bed in the bedroom the entire evening instead of coming out to the living room, which he always did until we would all go to bed. At 10:00 P.M., I had to wake Hank up so he could go outside before we all went to bed. It was very obvious that he still felt very bad about his accident. When he came back in from outside, he immediately got back on his bed and slept the entire night.

Hank usually slept all night and would want to go out around 7:00 A.M. He would then come back in, get on his bed, and wait for me to get dressed, after which I would take him back outside to eat. He usually just stayed on his bed until I came out of the bathroom. However, on this morning, after his accident, when I came out of the bathroom, Hank was not on his bed. He had gotten up and was over at the spot where he had his accident and was trying to clean the carpet. Hank was trying to clean up his mistake. Once again, Hank's actions indicated just how special he was and that he exhibited cognitive thinking and reasoning skills.

Hank had his first chemo treatment on Monday, March 4, 2013. We were told the first treatment could be hard on him; therefore, they wanted to keep him for the day in order to observe him. Seven percent of the dogs can experience side-effects from the chemo treatments such as vomiting and diarrhea, just like in humans. They don't lose their hair but they do lose their whiskers. At the end of the day, Hank seemed to be doing well, and we were told that we could come and get him. Jan and I watched him very closely on Tuesday, and again he seemed to be just fine. On Wednesday morning, however, he was very lethargic and did not want to eat. When Hank did not want to eat, we knew something was wrong. Jan suggested that maybe he would eat some canned dog food. We, as well as Herman, had always fed him dry dog food, which he seemed to really like. So for his evening meal, we gave him some canned dog food. It was around 4:00 P.M. when I fed him after he had laid around all day. He did show some interest in the canned dog food, which he ate along with a little dry food. Approximately thirty minutes later, Hank vomited all of his food. He also had had diarrhea in the afternoon. That was enough. We called Dr. Ehrlund and told her that Hank was experiencing side-effects. She requested that we bring Hank back to her in the morning. So on Thursday morning, back to Dr. Ehrlund's office we went.

Dr. Ehrlund kept Hank all day, giving him medicine for vomiting and diarrhea. We should have anticipated that he would be part of the 7 percent. Hank had always been very sensitive to just about everything. We had to give him medicine for allergies every day, so it should not have been a surprise to us that he would have side-effects from the chemotherapy. In addition to the medicine that Dr. Ehrlund gave him, she also gave him two intravenous bags of fluids in order to rehydrate him. At approximately 4:30 P.M., I called Dr. Ehrlund to see how Hank was doing. Dr. Ehrlund said he was much better and that we could come and get him. Of course, Jan and I did not waste any time getting over to her office. Hank was, indeed, much better and really enjoyed his supper that night. Dr. Ehrlund also provided us with some medicine to treat his vomiting and diarrhea.

For the next two weeks, Hank received his weekly chemo treatments on Monday. He seemed to tolerate chemo pretty well, and I only had to give him one pill for vomiting and one pill for diarrhea. It worked out that Hank would have one bad day each week, ranging from the third to the fifth day after the chemo treatments.

It was during his third week of treatment when Hank once again displayed his cognitive thinking abilities. I normally fed Hank once in the morning around 7:30 A.M. and once in the afternoon around 4:00 P.M. He would get one cup of dry dog food at each of his feedings. This routine for eating had satisfied him all of his life, and he was able to maintain his weight around sixty pounds, which was exactly the weight Dr. Ehrlund wanted him to have. Well, on one of the days during this time period, I had fed him his normal one cup in the morning. However, Hank got hungry around 2:00 P.M. in the afternoon, so I decided to feed him a little early. We were glad he was hungry since many times during this period, he was not that interested in his food. About two hours after he ate and Jan and I were watching TV, Hank got up from his bed in the living room and walked down from the rug in front of the sofa, where he stopped and looked at us, indicating he wanted something. He was looking directly at me this time. Since I had just fed him two hours earlier, we assumed he just needed to go out to potty. Since we thought that was what he wanted, Jan decided to get up and let him out even though he was obviously looking at me. Since we always let him out our bedroom door, Jan headed to the bedroom to let him out. Hank followed, but when he got to the door, he stopped and then returned to the living room, where I was. He again walked down the rug, stopped at the end, and again looked directly at me. This time he also gave me a "woof." I now knew he wanted me to take him out. So I got up and outside we went. Once outside, Hank went directly to his food bowls and then looked at the garage door. (I kept his dry dog food in the garage.) He then looked up at me as if to say, "Hey, dummy, I am still hungry." He was telling me that he was still hungry, and since I was the one who always fed him, he knew he had to get my attention—not Jan's. I went to the garage and got him another one-half cup of food. He immediately ate this additional food and then went back to the door to go back inside. Once again, Hank had communicated exactly what he wanted by insisting that I take him out and not Jan. When he just had to potty, either one of us could take him out. There was no doubt in either Jan's or my mind that Hank knew exactly what he wanted and from whom. Hank was always able to communicate his needs just like Herman had said: "He will let you know."

When we took Hank in for his fourth treatment the following week, we received some more bad news when we returned to pick him up. Dr. Ehrlund did not give him his treatment because she had found a large lump on the right side of his throat. I had noticed it on Saturday before the Monday appointment and was going to ask Dr. Ehrlund about it when we came back to pick him up. We did not see Dr. Ehrlund when we had dropped him off.

When we arrived at her office, the receptionist said Dr. Ehrlund wanted to talk to us. This was when she told us she thought something else was going on with Hank. She wanted us to take him to a veterinary specialist hospital to get a sonogram and x-ray of this lump. She made the appointment for the next Wednesday, March 27, 2013. The appointment was with Dr. Wiley at the South Texas Veterinary Specialist Hospital. Dr. Wiley specializes in cancer treatment for dogs.

We took Hank in to see Dr. Wiley on March 27, 2013. After examining Hank, she confirmed a large tumor was present on his right thyroid gland. She then performed a biopsy on this lump and confirmed it was cancerous. She also indicated that she thought the tumor was operable. However, she indicated that she wanted Hank to complete five more chemo treatments for his lymphoma before he underwent surgery on this tumor.

From March 27 to April 15, 2013, Hank had his weekly chemo treatments. However, he was now exhibiting side-effects of the chemo between Wednesday and Friday, after each of the Monday treatments. We had to take Hank in to see Dr. Ehrlund each week to get I.V.s since he would get dehydrated due to the vomiting and diarrhea. The I.V.s would always help him, and he was able to recover just in time for his next treatment.

On April 15, 2015, Dr. Ehrlund completed his usual blood test as part of his weekly treatment. On that day, we received the best news we could have when she happily informed us that Hank was "in remission"! We did continue with his chemo treatments to complete the five that Dr. Wiley had requested, after which Dr. Ehrlund scheduled Hank to return to Dr. Wiley on May 28, 2013.

During this appointment, Dr. Wiley examined Hank again and indicated that she could schedule Hank for his surgery the very next day: May 29, 2013. She had the surgeon, Dr. Fred Williams Jr., come in to talk to us about the surgery. Dr. Williams was very good about explaining what had to be done and indicated that he felt there was a very high probability that he could get the entire tumor out of his thyroid. We left Hank there so that he could be prepped for his surgery on Wednesday, May 29, 2013.

On Thursday, May 30, 2013, Dr. Williams called us to report that Hank's surgery had gone very well and that he had gotten the entire tumor. This was very good news to us. He also indicated that we could pick Hank up after 2:00 P.M. We happily arrived at the hospital that afternoon to pick Hank up to go home.

Hank had a very large bandage around his throat, which he was to keep on and clean for ten to twelve days (see photo 20). Hank was very good during this time period and did not try to disturb his bandage. It seemed that he knew he should not bother it (see photo 21).

On June 10, 2013, we took Hank back to Dr. Wiley to have his bandage removed. Dr. Wiley confirmed that indeed the entire thyroid tumor had been removed and that Hank had a good prognosis for a full recovery. She did indicate that Hank should continue with five more chemo treatments, but this time they could be every three weeks instead of weekly.

On June 17, 2013, Hank received the first of the five additional chemo treatments. Once again, on Wednesday following the treatment, Hank experienced significant side-effects from the chemo in the form of vomiting and diarrhea. We again had to take Hank in to see Dr. Ehrlund for I.V.s and injections. At least during this time period, Hank had three weeks to recover before he had to have the next treatment.

After the second treatment of the five, Hank really experienced significant side-effects. He lost his appetite and had significant diarrhea. We had to take him in on Thursday, July 11, 2013, to see Dr. Ehrlund. She began the normal I.V. treatment that had always worked in the past, but this time, it seemed that the I.V.s were not having much effect on Hank. In fact, at 3:00 P.M., Dr. Ehrlund called us and said she was going to keep him overnight. This was not good news for us.

On Friday afternoon, Dr. Ehrlund again called and said Hank was still not responding to the treatment, and she recommended that Hank go to Angel of Mercy Pet Hospital for the weekend since Hank was still experiencing a significant amount of diarrhea. Angel of Mercy has doctors on duty at nights and on weekends to care for pets.

It had now been almost two days since Jan and I had seen Hank and he had seen us. This was the longest time that either Jan or I had been away from Hank since he had come to live with us. We both missed him very much, and we knew Hank missed us. We knew he was wondering where his "mommy and daddy" were. We had always come back to pick him up from the vet on the days we had dropped him off.

On Saturday, Jan and I just had to go visit Hank at Angel of Mercy. They had regular visiting hours just like human hospitals. This was probably the very best thing we could have done for Hank.

The technician led us to one of the exam rooms and placed a pad on the floor for Hank. The technician then went to the back to get Hank. As Hank entered the room and saw us, the expression on Hank's face changed from one of despair to one of happiness. His "mommy and daddy" had come for him. He was very weak and immediately lay down on the pad the technician had placed on the floor for him. I got down on the floor and started petting him and talking to him. Jan moved a chair over close to us so she could also pet him. We "loved on" Hank for an hour while he slept or, at least, had his eyes closed. We did the same thing on Sunday. This was very therapeutic for all three of us. Hank missed us, and we missed him.

On Monday morning, July 15, 2013, we went back to Angel of Mercy to pick Hank up and take him back to Dr. Ehrlund's office. Hank was much better when he saw it was us, and the sparkle seemed to return to his eyes. He was, however, extremely weak and unsteady walking out to the truck. At Dr. Ehrlund's office, we weighed Hank and he was down to forty-eight pounds. He had lost twelve pounds, or 20 percent of his body weight, and was extremely weak. Dr. Ehrlund immediately placed him back on I.V.s.

At 4:00 that afternoon, Dr. Ehrlund called and said that Hank was better but remained weak. She did say that she thought he could come home if we could handle his diarrhea problems, which were slowly improving. Of course, Jan and I said we would be right over.

Over the next few days, Hank continued to improve and get stronger. Jan and I both firmly believe that our visits on Saturday and Sunday were the turning point for Hank. He knew we wanted him to get well, and he wanted to continue the fight to get better.

Hank had his next chemo treatment on July 29, 2013. Once again, the side-effects manifested themselves on the following Thursday. We again took Hank in for his I.V. treatment and injections. Dr. Ehrlund said she was going to call Dr. Wiley and see if there was some different medicine that we might be able to use that had fewer side-effects.

On August 19, 2013, Hank had his third chemo treatment. Once again, the side-effects occurred on the following Friday. Dr. Ehrlund was somewhat surprised since she and Dr. Wiley had reduced the dosage for his treatment. She gave Hank the I.V.s, and we picked him up at 4:00 P.M. and took him home. Over the next few days, he got a little better but continued to have diarrhea. Once again, Hank stopped eating and was getting dehydrated due to the diarrhea. We had to again take Hank in for additional I.V.s on Friday, August 30, 2013. When we picked Hank up later that day, Dr. Ehrlund said she would consult with Dr. Wiley to determine if the remaining chemo treatments were necessary since the treatments were becoming worse than the disease. He was scheduled for the next chemo treatment on September 9, 2013. On Friday, September 6, I called Dr. Ehrlund to see if Hank needed the treatment that was scheduled for Monday the ninth . She said to bring Hank in as scheduled and she would check him over.

On Monday, September 9, 2013, Jan and I took Hank in to see what the verdict was going to be. The last chemo treatment side-effects had lasted the entire three-week period between treatments. Dr. Ehrlund examined Hank, took a blood sample, and checked his heart and lungs. As we waited patiently in the exam room with Hank, all three of us were hoping for the best. After analyzing the blood sample, Dr. Ehrlund came back into the room and said that Hank was still in remission and that his heart and lungs all sounded strong. She also said that he also did not have any more lumps in his lymphoid. His weight was also back up to sixty pounds. Because of this, she said she did not need to see Hank again for six months unless he became ill again. This was great news for all of us. Hank had conquered two types of cancer! From the four-to-six-week diagnosis of life on February 27, 2013, Hank had reached six months of life on August 27, 2013. God's guiding hand had been with Hank, our "Angel Dog." As we departed for home, Jan and I knew we would enjoy and cherish each and every day and every additional moment that God was going to allow us to have with Hank. We hoped that Hank would also exceed the normal average of ten to twelve months of life expectancy for these types of cancer.

As a side note, the day Hank started his initial chemo treatments, another dog that had cancer was also started on chemo with Dr. Ehrlund. Before we left her office with our good news, we asked how the other dog was doing. She was sorry to say that this dog did not make it. God's hand was with Hank.

# Chapter 7

# "Angel Dog, Miracle Dog"

Hank was not only an "Angel Dog"; he was also a "Miracle Dog." One evening during November of 2013, Hank was expressing great difficulty getting up from his bed. When he did finally get up, he had trouble walking in a straight line. He was leaning to the left and would run into the wall or doorframe on the left as he tried to go outside to potty. Once outside in the backyard, he was only able to walk around in circles to the left, and his head was tilted to the left side. Jan and I knew immediately that we needed to take him in to see Dr. Ehrlund, as something was very seriously wrong with Hank. We called her office the next morning, and of course, she said to bring him right in.

After Dr. Ehrlund examined Hank, she said that Hank had suffered a small stroke. She said that most of his symptoms would go away in a couple of weeks, but his head may not straighten out. We took Hank home to comfort him, feeling happy that he was still alive but waiting to see just how much he would recover.

By December 2013, Hank had improved significantly. Most of his symptoms had gone away. Even his head tilt to the left was getting better. By January 2014, the tilt of his head to the left was hardly noticeable. Hank was essentially back to normal. During this time period, from February 2013 to December 2013, Hank had conquered two types of cancer and survived a stroke. Truly Hank was a "Miracle Dog."

It was also during December 2013 that we received Hank's records from the time he had spent at Angel of Mercy Hospital in July 2013. The doctor's notes from the hospital confirmed that our visits on Saturday and Sunday, July

13 and 14, had indeed been the turning point for Hank. The notes from his stay on July 11 and 12, 2013 (Thursday and Friday), indicated that he was depressed and was not eating. After our visits with him on the thirteenth and fourteenth, he was no longer described as being depressed, and he began to eat. These notes did confirm exactly what Jan and I already knew, that our visits were the turning point for Hank. He knew we still loved him and wanted him to get well and come home. When Hank saw us on those days, he knew we had not deserted him, and the expression on his face told us how happy he was and that he was going to fight through those difficult times. His comeback had begun on July 13 and 14, which was the low point of his battle against cancer as we had suspected. We now had written proof.

Also during January 2014, Hank really wanted to go for his morning walk at the park when he was able. He soon developed a group of well-wishers at the park. There were four women at the park who walked their dogs each day. They took an interest in Hank and would always ask about him each time they saw him. They were always very happy when we could report that he was doing well and expressed concern when he was not feeling well. Then on February 27, 2014, these ladies, led by Carol, presented Hank with a card and a goodie bag of treats to celebrate his one-year anniversary since being diagnosed with cancer. They also began to call him a "Miracle Dog." They were correct. Hank had overcome two types of cancer and a stroke in order to live. Hank was not only an "Angel Dog" but a "Miracle Dog" as well.

When Hank reached the one-year survival point, which was maximum average time for dog cancer survivors, we were extremely happy. We knew that God's hand was still guiding Hank's life.

When March 2014 arrived, Hank was fifteen years and six months old. He continued to do well and amaze us with his thinking skills and actions. As I have mentioned, it was always the little things he did that amazed us so much. Another example of his thinking skills was evidenced by the following.

I had always been interested in coin collecting; however, after I retired for the second time, I became a serious coin collector. One day late in February 2014, when I was working with my coin collection, I had removed a number of coin display cases from the gun cabinet, where I stored them. I had taken these display cases out and had placed them on the floor in our bedroom, where Hank liked to roll. Jan and I were both out in the living room when Hank decided he wanted to roll on the carpet in our bedroom. He liked the carpet in our bedroom. He liked the carpet back there to roll on because we have hardwood flooring in the living room. We did not think much about Hank going back there since he did it quite often. Soon after his departure to the bedroom, we heard Hank barking loudly as if something was wrong. We both immediately went back to see what was bothering Hank. When we got back to the bedroom, there was Hank, standing and barking in the middle of the coin display boxes. I had placed my display boxes in the area where he liked to roll. Hank was expressing his great displeasure about my choice of placement of the display boxes. Jan and I both laughed at Hank, and of course, I put the display boxes back in the gun cabinet. Hank watched and waited patiently for me to finish, and then he began to roll. Hank once again amazed us with his actions and communication skills. Once again, we remembered Herman's famous words: "He will let you know."

# Chapter 8

# The End

It was just a few days into March 2014, after the barking incident with the coin display boxes, when we noticed that Hank began to slow down. On his morning walks, he started to walk very slowly and did not seem to have much endurance. We took Hank in to see Dr. Ehrlund and have her examine him. After checking him over, she said he did have a slight murmur and his blood pressure was slightly elevated, but everything else seemed to be okay. She put him on some medicine for his blood pressure and said that she wanted to check him again in a week.

We took him back on March 27, 2014, to have his blood pressure checked. This time it was normal, and Hank seemed to be doing well. He was eating well, wanted to go on his morning walks, and seemed to be much stronger.

Then on Saturday, April 5, 2014, Hank vomited three times during the day and did not want to eat. On Sunday, April 6, 2014, he was much better, eating well and wanting to go for his walk. On Monday, April 7, he was even better, stronger, eating well, and even wanting to walk farther than normal. On Tuesday, April 8, he was even better. By Wednesday, April 9, Hank was the strongest he had been in a very long time and did the best he had done on his morning walk in a long time. Even Carol, his friend at the park, noticed how well Hank was doing when she gave him his treats. (She always had treats for Hank.) Jan and I were very happy with how well he was doing.

During the day on Wednesday, Hank just slept like he normally did after his walk. At 4:00 P.M., he was hungry and told me it was time for him to eat.

He ate well and did not seem to be having any problems walking, nor was he experiencing any other type of discomfort. At 6:30 P.M., he wanted to go outside to potty; however, when he got up, his back legs seemed to fail him and he fell back down. I helped him up, and he finally was able to go outside. While outside in the backyard, he seemed to be having difficulty going potty. It looked as if he was constipated and was having a significant amount of trouble having a bowel movement. He did finally come back in to the house and slept on his bed until around 9:30 P.M. When I woke him up again to go outside before we all went to bed, he was very weak but was able to get up and go outside. While outside, he once again had great difficulty going potty. When he did come back in, he lay down on his bed and remained in this position as he went to sleep. He normally would get up and turn around to put his head on his pillow, but he did not do that this time. His breathing also became somewhat labored as he slept, but he did not seem to be in any pain, so Jan and I went to bed. I was concerned since Hank had been so strong during the day and now seemed to be very weak.

At 3:00 A.M., Hank got me up to go outside. He was able to get up, but he seemed very weak. He did go outside but again was having trouble having a bowel movement. Upon returning to his bed, he just seemed to collapse, and his breathing became even more labored. I was really becoming concerned about Hank. I was so concerned that I stayed on the floor with him for forty-five minutes to an hour, petting him and giving him comfort. His breathing continued to be labored, but he did finally go to sleep. I returned to bed, thinking that if we did not see any improvement in the morning, we would have to take him in to see Dr. Ehrlund.

I got up around 7:30 A.M. on Thursday, April 10, 2014. Hank had not moved from the position I had left him in at 4:00 A.M. I told Jan we were taking Hank in to see Dr. Ehrlund. I called her office at 8:10 A.M. to see if she had any appointment openings that morning. This was when I knew God was again looking over Hank. Dr. Ehrlund had her first appointment time of the day (9:00 A.M.) open. We left immediately.

Hank was not able to get up on his own, so I carried him out to the truck and placed him on the back seat. He did not move from that position during the trip to see Dr. Ehrlund. When we got to her office, I carried Hank inside. The staff at Dr. Ehrlund's office had prepared a pad for Hank in one of the exam rooms. I placed Hank on the pad, and we waited for Dr. Ehrlund to come in.

Dr. Ehrlund came in as soon as she knew Hank was there. She immediately got down on the floor with Hank to examine him. She noted that Hank had a lot of fluid in his abdominal cavity. She did not know if the fluid was from his liver or his heart. She also checked his reflexes and indicated that she thought something may be going on in his back or his liver. She said that she was going to take some x-rays to see if she could see anything that was causing his discomfort.

We waited while Hank was x-rayed. When Dr. Ehrlund came back in, she said there was too much fluid to see anything in his abdominal cavity. She indicated that she wanted to run some blood tests and get a sonogram of his abdominal cavity. She said she would keep him and would call us in the afternoon with the results. She also said if it was just fluid and nothing else, she could treat him and get him back. Jan and I left around 10:00 A.M., hoping for the best.

At 4:00 P.M., Dr. Ehrlund called with the results. The news was not good. She indicated that the sonogram had revealed that Hank had two large tumors in his abdomen. One tumor was located on his liver. It was so large, in fact, that Dr. Ehrlund said it was the largest tumor she had seen! The other tumor was located under his diaphragm and was pushing upward. This was the cause of his labored breathing. She then said there was not anything she could do for Hank. She said he would not be able to ever walk again and he would not be able to eat again. I asked if he was suffering. She said she did not think he was yet, but it was only a matter of hours before we would be suffering. Her recommendation was that we should put him down now so that he would not suffer or go through any other indignities. Jan and I reluctantly agreed since we did not want Hank to suffer. We told Dr. Ehrlund that we would be right over.

During the day while Hank was with Dr. Ehrlund, I had been thinking about an email we had received from someone back in 2009. I had saved a copy of the email because I liked it so much. The email was titled "A Pet's Ten Commandments." The tenth commandment was the following:

> "On the ultimate difficult journey, go with me, please. Never say you can't bear to watch. Don't make me face this alone. Everything is easier for me if you are there, because I love you so."

I knew I could not let Hank face his final journey alone.

Dr. Ehrlund met us at the door of her office and took us back to Hank. He was lying on the pad they had provided him. Dr. Ehrlund said we could have as much time with him as we needed to say our goodbyes. I lay down on the floor close to Hank with my face just a few inches away from his. We both looked into each other's eyes as I talked to him while petting him. Jan got a chair and placed it next to Hank so that she could pet him, too.

After about thirty minutes, Dr. Ehrlund returned and asked if we were ready. We reluctantly indicated we were. I continued to pet Hank while looking into his big brown eyes as Dr. Ehrlund administered the medicine. It was only a minute or two when Dr. Ehrlund said, "He is gone." She said we could have some more time with him and she would return to check his heart.

When she did return, she confirmed that Hank had passed. Our "Angel/Miracle Dog" had returned to heaven. Hank's time on earth had ended, and God had taken him home to heaven to be reunited with Herman. God had definitely guided Hank's entire life here on Earth until his return to heaven on April 10, 2014, after fifteen years and seven months.

We told Dr. Ehrlund that we were going to bury Hank at Mission Park South Pet Cemetery on Monday, April 14, 2014. She said she would take care of him for us until Monday.

When we picked Hank up on Monday, we were amazed how Dr. Ehrlund had prepared him to look like he was just sleeping. We took him home so that I could place him in his casket. In his casket, I had placed his favorite bed with the built-in pillow on it. Jan had bought a new purple towel to cover his bed. He always liked new towels (see photo 22). I then laid him in his casket and placed his favorite toy with him. The casket came with a satin pillow and a satin sheet to place over him (see photo 23).

On Monday, April 14, 2014, at 3:00 P.M., Hank was buried as Jan and I said our final goodbyes. We had a headstone made for his grave so that all would know that Hank was an "Angel Dog" (see photo 24). Hank was truly an "Angel Dog," a blessing from God.

# Conclusion

Jan and I had no doubt in our minds that Hank was indeed an "Angel Dog." He obviously was placed here on Earth by God for a very specific purpose. It was also obvious that his life was guided by God's hands in order for him to fulfill that purpose. His life was saved four times.

The first time was when Byron and Herman rescued him from the animal shelter in Omaha. God guided Byron and Herman to that shelter on that specific day to rescue Hank for Herman. God knew that Herman would need help to get through the loss of his wife. Hank was the means that God provided to ease Herman's pain. In addition, Hank needed Herman to recover from the abuse he had obviously suffered as a puppy.

When we got Hank, God guided us to Dr. Ehrlund. We did not have a veterinarian when we brought Hank home to Texas with us. We happened to be at a Texas A&M football game when we saw a couple from San Antonio who worked with Jan at her school district. As we talked, we mentioned that we had just acquired Hank. The subject of a vet came up, and this couple told us about Dr. Ehrlund. They could not say enough about how good of a veterinarian she was and she was a graduate of Texas A&M. Being Aggie parents, this was good enough for Jan and me. Dr. Ehrlund was going to be Hank's doctor. It was even better that she was a woman since Hank never had any problems with females. God knew who Hank needed to be his doctor.

Dr. Ehrlund saved Hank's life three times. The first time was the removal of the rope from his stomach and two times due to the two types of cancer he had. We could tell God was guiding Hank's life just by the way things worked out timing wise to ensure that his life was saved.

Hank was such a special dog. He brought so much happiness to Herman and then to Jan and me. He was very important member of our family. A day never went by without Hank doing something to put a smile on our faces and our hearts.

When we told Herman about the things Hank did after he came to live with us, he would just say, "Nothing would surprise me about Hank."

Hank was that type of special dog that only comes along once in a lifetime. You just had to live with Hank to fully appreciate just how special he was. Everyone who met Hank or observed him could tell he was indeed an exceptional dog. When I informed Hank's friend Carol and her friends at the park of Hank's death, we all shed tears. Even our next-door neighbor cried when I told him Hank had passed away. Dr. Ehrlund and her staff placed a memorial tribute to Hank on their veterinary website. Hank was truly an "Angel Dog/Miracle Dog" and a blessing to all who knew him.

# Epilogue

It was about six months after Hank was diagnosed with cancer when I happened to notice a book in one of the many sales catalogs that we seem to receive in the mail. The book was titled *I Will See You in Heaven*, by Friar Jack Wintz. It had a picture of a dog on the cover, and it piqued my curiosity. I somehow always hoped there would be dogs in heaven, but I had never read anything that discussed it. Naturally, I just had to read this book.

In the book, Friar Wintz provided biblical references that God always intended for us to have our pets with us in heaven. This book also confirmed to me that Hank was an "Angel Dog" and that God had guided Hank's life while he was here on Earth.

As I looked back over Hank's life after reading this book, I could clearly see God's hand guiding Hank to fulfill his purpose here on Earth. God had provided the path for Hank to be part of our family. He had allowed Hank to get lost as a puppy and end up in the Omaha Shelter to be present on the very day my mother-in-law passed away. He led Byron and Herman to stop at the shelter on that very day while looking for a dog for Herman. God provided the perfect companion for Herman during his great time of need for comfort. This was evidenced by an email from Byron when we informed him of Hank's passing. God's hand was in evidence in Byron's words when he responded with the following:

> *I think of when we found him in the kennel, and although he wasn't the hunting variety that Dad had always lived with,*

*(Hank) seemed to be the perfect one. When I took him on the leash into the big open field, they told me to hold on to him because he was very nervous and would try to run off. He never strayed more than two feet from me. When he got back to the kennel, he stayed by my side and didn't want to leave me. It was a special bond that extended from that time to our entire family. His loyalty to Dad was a wonderful thing that enriched Dad's later years so much. Then his transition to you (Jan) and Dave was just a wonderful time for him and you. He had a great life after leaving that kennel, and he gave so much back to all of us who loved him. I expect that he is sitting up there with Dad now and when he hears that loud command, "Hank, get in here!" he will respond dutifully and with a big smile on his face.*

Only God could have led Hank to us. God's guiding hand can also be seen when I was led to let Herman know that Jan and I would be happy to take care of Hank if he was not able to do so. There was no indication at that time that such a situation would ever arise when I brought up the subject. This had to have been part of God's plan for Hank.

God also led us to Dr. Ehrlund here in San Antonio. We did not know any veterinarians at the time we got Hank. God led us to the couple who did know the perfect vet for Hank at a most unlikely place: a Texas A&M football game. Dr. Ehrlund played a very important part in God's plan for Hank.

God was with Hank when he swallowed the knot on the end of the rope while we were gone. Only God could have helped him swallow it without choking himself to death. That knot was the size of a lemon and also had some of the rope itself attached. Even Dr. Ehrlund could not believe what Hank had done.

God's presence was also evidenced at the time he was diagnosed with cancer. We had taken him in for his annual checkup in January of 2013. He got an excellent report from Dr. Ehrlund with only the recommendation to get his teeth cleaned. If the local rodeo had not been starting the next week, we would have scheduled him for his teeth cleaning. By waiting until the end of the rodeo, which was thirty days, Dr. Ehrlund was able to diagnose the Stage III Lymphoma cancer. If we would have gotten his teeth cleaned the very next week after his checkup, we might not have detected the cancer in time to treat it. This had to be part of God's plan for Hank as far as timing goes.

God then stepped in to heal Hank of the lymphoma, the thyroid cancer, and even a stroke. God was with Hank his entire life. Even when his time was up, God took care of Hank to keep him from suffering. Hank was strong right up to the last twelve hours, when he lost the use of his back legs. It was obvious that God was taking care of Hank because when I called Dr. Ehrlund's office at 8:10 A.M. on April 10, 2014, to see if she had any open appointments, her first appointment (9:00 A.M.) was available. God also allowed us time later that day to say our goodbyes. God guided Hank's whole life for fifteen years and seven months.

After reading Friar Wintz's book, and looking back over Hank's life, I know that Hank is in heaven, and we will get to see him again.

I mentioned in the book that I remembered the tenth commandment of "A Pet's Ten Commandments." I do not know who wrote them or even who emailed them to us in 2009. However, the following are the "Pet's Ten Commandments," and I can see Hank in every one of them.

1. My life is likely to last 10-15 years. Any separation from you is likely to be painful.
2. Give me time to understand what you want from me.
3. Place your trust in me. It is crucial for my wellbeing.
4. Don't be angry with me for long and don't lock me up as punishment. You have your work, your friends, your entertainment, but I have only you.
5. Talk to me. Even if I don't understand your words, I do understand your voice when speaking to me.
6. Be aware that however you treat me, I will never forget it.
7. Before you hit me, before you strike me, remember that I could hurt you, and yet, I choose not to bite you.
8. Before you scold me for being lazy or uncooperative, ask yourself if something might be bothering me. Perhaps I'm not getting the right food, I have been in the sun too long, or my heart might be getting old or weak.
9. Please take care of me when I grow old. You too will grow old.
10. On the ultimate difficult journey, go with me, please. Never say you can't bear to watch. Don't make me face this alone. Everything is easier for me if you are there, because I love you so."

We should all take a moment each day to thank God for our pets and to take good care of them. Life would be much duller and less joyful without part of God's creation.

*Photo 1: The white dog with a black patch around his right eye. The "Angel Dog".*

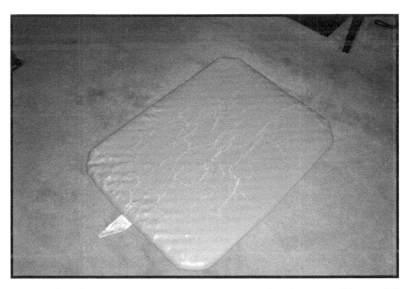

*Photo 2: A first for Herman. He bought Hank this pad to sleep on in Herman's bedroom. For seventy years, Herman only had outside dogs.*

*Photo 3: You can see that Hank's confidence has been restored in this photo.*

*Photo 4: You can see the bond between Hank and Herman by their body language.*

*Photo 5: Hank riding up front in the truck. Notice the confidence of Hank.*

*Photo 6: Hank sitting in the corner of the backyard waiting for Herman to return. He would wait for hours in this position.*

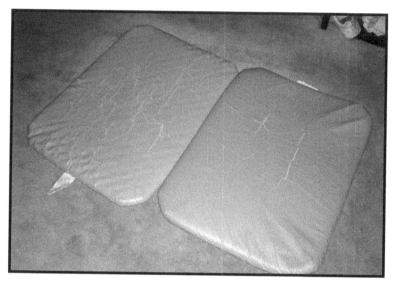

*Photo 7: I found a pad to match the one Herman bought Hank which became his bed.*

*Photo 8: Hank's bed consisted of a beach towel over the two pads that Herman and I had bought for him.*

*Photo 9: I found the perfect bed for Hank. It even had a pillow on it for his head.*

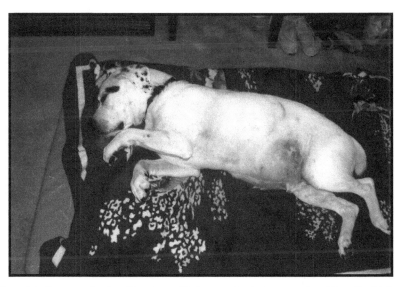

*Photo 10: During the day Hank would sleep on his bed using the pillow for his head without moving the towel.*

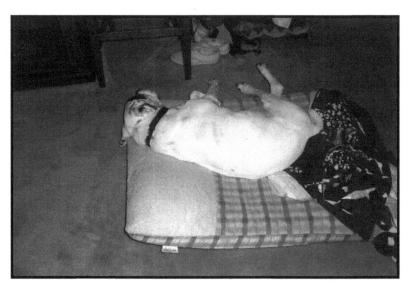

*Photo 11: At night Hank would pull the cover back on his bed just like us and then go to sleep.*

*Photo 12: Hank's Family Room bed which he also liked.*

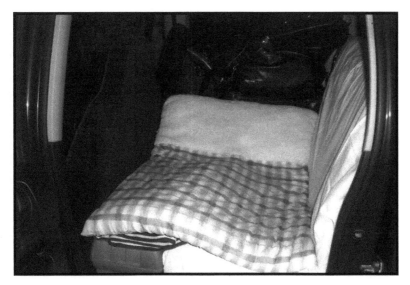

*Photo 13: Hank's bed in the back seat of the truck when we traveled.*

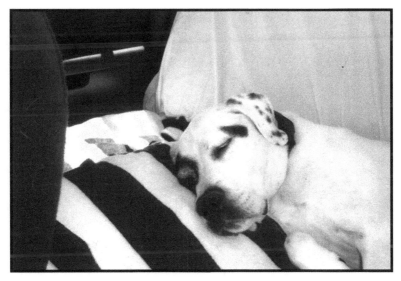

*Photo 14: Hank sleeping while we traveled.*

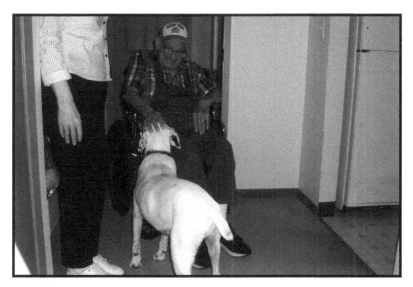

*Photo 15: Hank going over to Herman and placing his head on Herman's thigh. The smile on Herman's face was priceless.*

*Photo 16: Hank coming over to Herman as if to say, "I will never forget you."*

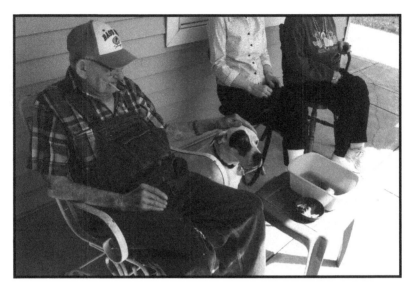

*Photo 17: Hank sitting by Herman on Herman's back porch of his apartment.*

*Photo 18: The bag with the piece of rope in it that Dr. Ehrlund had removed from Hank's stomach.*

*Photo 19: Hank strapped in with the seatbelts in the back seat of the truck.*

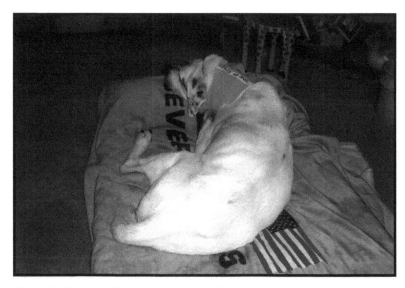

*Photo 20: Hank and his large bandage after tumor removal from his thyroid.*

*Photo 21: Hank made no attempt to remove his bandage after surgery.*

*Photo 22: Hank lying in his casket on his favorite bed with a new towel. He looked like he was just sleeping.*

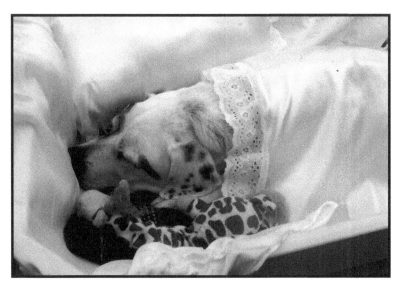

*Photo 23: Hank lying in his casket with his favorite toy, satin pillow and satin sheet over him.*

*Photo 24: Hank's headstone for all to know that he was truly an "Angel Dog".*